an illustrated introduction to
ANCIENT EGYPT

Charlotte Booth

AMBERLEY

Hapy, god of the inundation, Medinet Habu.

First published 2014

Amberley Publishing
The Hill, Stroud
Gloucestershire, GL5 4EP

www.amberley-books.com

British Library Cataloguing in Publication Data.
A catalogue record for this book is available from the British Library.

ISBN 978 1 4456 3365 7 (paperback)
ISBN 978 1 4456 3377 0 (ebook)

Typesetting and Origination by Amberley Publishing.
Printed in Great Britain.

CONTENTS

ANCIENT EGYPT
IN FIVE MINUTES

Everyone has some knowledge of or ideas about ancient Egypt, even if they have never studied it, or watched documentaries about it. Such knowledge includes the pyramids and how they were built, mummies, Tutankhamun and gold. Others may be able to add to this list Ramses II, unusual-looking gods and Cleopatra. All of these things are perfectly valid in the study of ancient Egypt, but there is so much more to it.

Egyptologists are lucky, as there is so much evidence available that most aspects of Egyptian life can be reconstructed. This is why in this book, rather than approach the history of Egypt in a chronological way, starting at the beginning of civilisation and moving through to Cleopatra and the Romans, I have chosen to approach it differently. Egyptian civilisation is not just about buildings, kings and mummies. Primarily civilisation is comprised of people who form the community and this is the approach adopted in the following pages. Each chapter looks at a different aspect of how the Egyptian people lived.

To understand the Egyptian people it is important to be able to visualise the world they lived in, and this is tackled in chapter 1, where the environment they lived in is introduced. The focus was obviously the River Nile, the source of all life, and the river's behaviour greatly affected all aspects of Egyptian life. This chapter will also explain the political divisions of Egypt and how the country was managed. Throughout most of the dynastic period Egypt was ruled by a single king, and the importance and origin of ruling a unified Egypt was fundamental to the ideology of kingship.

Archaeology has luckily unearthed numerous cities and villages dating as far back as 3500 BCE, and the most important capital cities, spanning 3,000 years of history, are discussed in the first chapter, which introduces some of the most interesting things about these cities.

Opposite: Lotus column, Karnak Temple. (Photograph courtesy of BKB Photography)

Chapter 3 looks at three settlements in further detail: el Lahun, Deir el Medina and Tell el Amarna. It introduces some of the characters who lived there through their letters and their fastidious record keeping, as well as through the houses they lived in. The information available about these people is remarkable. Have you ever called in sick from work? Well, so did the Egyptians. Have you ever got drunk and done something foolish? Well, so did the Egyptians. Have you ever been frustrated when someone ignored a letter and then claimed they never received it? Well, so did the Egyptians. Turn to chapter 3 to learn more about these day-to-day activities.

The Egyptians worked hard and played hard, and evidence of how they passed the time is presented. Eating was high on their list of fun activities, although in Egyptian artwork all of the women are beautifully thin, and the men are generally shown at the prime of life, perhaps with a couple of stylised rolls of fat. In our modern world, where diets are commonplace and people care greatly about their weight to the point of making themselves ill with anorexia or bulimia, it is hard to imagine a time when diets did not exist. Egypt was in constant fear of famine and therefore dieting would not have been considered sensible. Most people, therefore, were naturally slim. However, in artwork, in order to show wealth, men had a roll or two of fat added around their middle, indicating they were eating well. Women, however, were rarely shown as 'fat', although one image at Deir el Bahri of the Queen of Punt shows a very large woman, and has caused a great deal of discussion. On the whole women were depicted with a slim build, but sometimes with accentuated hips to emphasise their fertility, especially during the Amarna period.

In order to truly understand how the ancient Egyptian mind worked it is essential to turn to religion, which governed a great deal of the Egyptian lifestyle. There were hundreds of Egyptian deities, although they were not all worshipped at the same time in the same place. Religion, like culture, was changing constantly, and some gods were fashionable only at certain times, or were only appropriate for certain issues. In chapter 2 the main myths are discussed, as well as some of the key deities in the pantheon. Some deities were unique to certain places; for example Meretseger, 'She Who Loves Silence', worshipped at Deir el Medina, Luxor, or Sobek the crocodile god, worshipped at Kom Ombo in the south. Other deities were unique to individual families, comprising deceased relatives. As you can imagine, it is impossible to include every god in the pantheon in a book of this length, therefore I have focussed on the most important deities such as Osiris, Isis, Amun and Hathor.

Gods were essential for every aspect of life, including childbirth and medicine, and gods were called upon to help out in any given situation. We learn more about this practical application of religion in chapters 4 and 5, which form a 'cradle to the grave' scenario. Chapter 4 starts with childhood, explaining the normality of an Egyptian childhood, and how it is recognisable and comparable to a modern childhood. Children played with toys, created dangerous games involving jumping or running, and enjoyed model making and playing ball games. The toys discovered have truly stood the test of time, and modern versions of them exist: rag dolls, dolls and animals with articulated limbs, and leather balls. Childhood all too quickly led to teenage years, which in ancient Egypt was often marked by love and marriage. As one would expect, marriage was not long followed by pregnancy, even with the use of crocodile-dung contraceptives, and then ultimately childbirth. Turn to chapter 4 to learn about how the Egyptians marked these rites of passage and which gods were appealed to in times of need.

The final chapter investigates disease, retirement and death. The medical papyri that outline diseases and their cures make terrifying reading, especially when a doctor's medical kit includes broken glass for eye treatments. No wonder they appealed to the gods for help. Due to poor health and a lack of antibiotics old age started early, and many people died before their fortieth birthday.

Unfortunately, as much of the archaeological evidence comes from funerary contexts, many people have the wrong impression about the Egyptians. Rather than being obsessed with death and preparing for it their entire lives, the Egyptians loved life, and the preparations for the afterlife were a means by which to live for eternity. Mummification and grave goods were a way of ensuring the deceased would have a body and their belongings to use in the afterlife. This final chapter investigates what the Egyptians expected in death and the afterlife.

This brief introduction will enable you to gain an insight into the lives of the ancient Egyptians while learning about their environment, kingship, and village life. Read on to discover more.

TIMELINE

Pre-Dynastic Period

	Before 3050 BCE

Early Dynastic Period

Dynasty 0	3150–3050 BCE
Dynasty 1	3050–2890 BCE
Dynasty 2	2890–2686 BCE

Old Kingdom

Dynasty 3	2686–2613 BCE
Dynasty 4	2613–2500 BCE
Dynasty 5	2498–2345 BCE
Dynasty 6	2345–2333 BCE

First Intermediate Period

Dynasty 7 and 8	2180–2160 BCE
Dynasty 9 and 10	2160–2040 BCE

Middle Kingdom

Dynasty 11	2134–1991 BCE
Dynasty 12	1991–1782 BCE

Second Intermediate Period

Dynasty 13	1782–1650 BCE
Dynasty 14	?
Dynasty 15	1663–1555 BCE
Dynasty 16	1663–1555 BCE
Dynasty 17	1663–1570 BCE

New Kingdom

Dynasty 18	1570–1293 BCE
Dynasty 19	1308–1185 BCE
Dynasty 20	1185–1070 BCE

Third Intermediate Period

High Priests (Thebes)	1080–945 BCE
Dynasty 21 (Tanis)	1069–945 BCE
Dynasty 22 (Tanis)	945–715 BCE
Dynasty 23 (Leontopolis)	818–715 BCE
Dynasty 24 (Sais)	727–715 BCE
Dynasty 25 (Nubians)	747–656 BCE
Dynasty 26 (Sais)	664–525 BCE

Late Period

Dynasty 27 (Persian)	525–404 BCE
Dynasty 28	404–399 BCE
Dynasty 29	399–380 BCE
Dynasty 30	380–343 BCE
Dynasty 31	343–332 BCE

Graeco-Roman Period

Macedonian Kings	332–305 BCE
Ptolemaic Period	305–30 BCE

GLOSSARY OF USEFUL TERMS

Book of the Dead   A New Kingdom funerary text made up of a number of independent chapters. These chapters were used to decorate tombs, coffins, bandages and papyri. It was not necessary to use the entire text for it to be effective.

canopic jars   These were the four jars used to accommodate the mummified internal organs of the deceased. Each head represented one of the sons of Horus.

cartouche   This is the oval shape which surrounds the name of the king. It is also sometimes used for important queens' names and the name of the god Aten.

faience   A commonly used material, rather like ceramic, made from powdered quartz, which can be glazed in bright colours. Before being fired it can be moulded into any required shape.

hieratic   Hieratic was the shorthand version of hieroglyphics and was used for all non-religious documents. It was always written from right to left.

inundation   Annually the Nile flooded from June to September, covering Egypt in rich, black, fertile silt.

ka   The life force of a human, present throughout their lives. It is represented as a 'twin' of the individual, often with a pair of arms upon its head.

Lower Egypt   The north of Egypt.

Maat   Maat was the goddess of truth and justice, but the word simply means 'truth' and was used as a means of describing justice and cosmic equilibrium. It was important to live according to the laws of Maat. Judges were often priests of Maat.

mastaba   This tomb type was common in the Old Kingdom. The word comes from the Arabic for 'bench' in reference to the box-shaped, rectangular appearance of the tomb superstructure.

natron   The natural salt which came from the Wadi Natron, and was used in cooking, drying food and mummification.

ostraca   Limestone chips or pottery fragments were used by the ancient Egyptians as notepaper. They range in size from a few centimetres to over a metre long. They have been found in their thousands and cover laundry lists, blueprints for tombs and even literary texts.

Pyramid Texts   These religious texts first appear in the pyramid of Unas (fifth dynasty). They are made up of a number of utterances or spells that help the deceased king in the afterlife. It was not necessary to have all of the texts in one place, or in order.

Upper Egypt   The south of Egypt.

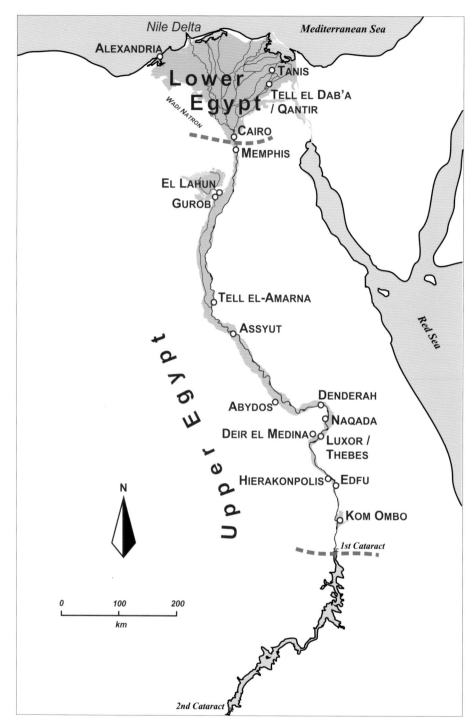

Map of Egypt. Kindly produced by Peter Robinson.

1

THE EGYPTIAN ENVIRONMENT

The phrase 'ancient Egypt' immediately conjures up images of mummies, gold, pyramids and anthropomorphic gods. While these things are certainly important aspects of ancient Egyptian history, there is so much more to it, with many elements of daily, political and economic life available for study.

Ancient Egypt is often presented as a static culture, whereas its history actually covers a period of approximately 3,500 years, from the start of the settled civilisation to the Roman occupation. There are also thousands of years of nomadic history prior to this, and 2,000 years of history after, which are equally important but do not generally come under the banner of Egyptology. During these 3,500 years the culture was not static, and beliefs, practices, culture, art and language changed over the centuries. Therefore, a comprehensive guide to the history of Egypt would require many volumes and a lifetime of research, but this book will provide an overview of these 3,500 years, using cultural aspects that were consistent over the period. For time-specific information, dates will be provided.

CHRONOLOGY

Dates spanning back so many thousands of years create a number of problems, and often there are discrepancies between different books and scholars. This can partly be blamed on the Egyptians themselves, as they did not have a centralised dating system. Their dating system revolved around a king's reign, starting at year one whenever a new king came to the throne. However, they did not often record the date of the king's death, meaning there is no accurate way of knowing how long each king ruled for, what year he died in and consequently when the first year of the next king started.

Egyptian chronology, therefore, is constantly evolving, as assumptions can only be made about a king's reign length from the last known date taken from tombs, temples, and wine jars. This is problematic for two main reasons. It is not always clear if a king co-ruled with another king, meaning that sometimes reign dates overlapped. Another problem is Egyptian record keeping. Some kings, in an attempt to erase unfavourable kings from history, simply added their reign length to those of any erased kings. For example, official inscriptions indicate Amenhotep III was followed on the throne by Horemheb. However, between these two kings, Akhenaten, Tutankhamun and Ay reigned for a period of approximately twenty-nine years. Horemheb's reign length was sometimes recorded as a sum of all of these kings added to his own.

New evidence is discovered annually that changes reign lengths and alters the chronology of Egypt. This results in each publication using a different set of dates, depending on whether the author agrees with theories of reign lengths and co-regencies, and how old their source books are. Throughout this book the dates used are from Peter Clayton's *Chronicle of the Pharaohs*.

DYNASTIES

It is far easier to use dynasties rather than chronological dates when discussing Egyptian history. The Pharaonic period is divided into thirty-one dynasties, ideally with each representing one family of royal descent, although this is not always the case. These dynastic divisions were not, however, introduced or even used by the ancient Egyptians themselves. They believed the royal line was traceable to the gods through their divine nature, and therefore they were all part of the same bloodline.

This system was introduced by Manetho in the third century BCE in an attempt to organise the kings. This system has been adopted by all Egyptologists. The dynasties were divided into three main periods: the Old Kingdom, the Middle Kingdom and the New Kingdom. Between each of these main epochs was a period of political unrest and economic instability known as an intermediate period – specifically the First, Second and Third Intermediate Periods. The end of the Third Intermediate Period saw the start of the rather unstable Late Period, characterised by Persian and Libyan invasions and Amun priests on the throne.

The invasion of Alexander the Great in 332 BCE saw the start of a dynasty of rulers known as the Ptolemaic period, comprising fifteen kings called Ptolemy and two queens, Berenice IV and Cleopatra VII. The latter was the last ruler of Egypt before the Romans conquered in 30 BCE.

While Manetho's method of recording the kings is useful, it does not account for a pre-dynastic period, which was only discovered in the 1890s, meaning a new dynasty was added: Dynasty 0. It also does not accommodate 'new' kings discovered since its creation. For example, in January 2014 a new king's name, Woseribre Senebkay, was discovered in a tomb south of Abydos dated to the Second Intermediate Period. The chronology will once more need to be adjusted to accommodate this new king.

THE NILE

The most important (and consistent) aspect of ancient Egypt was the River Nile, as without it the Egyptians would not have survived in the harsh desert environment. That was as true for ancient as it is for modern Egyptians. The river flows from south to north, and is the longest river in the world, at 6,650 kilometres long, running through four countries including Egypt. Due to this direction of flow, southern Egypt was called Upper Egypt (being closest to the source of the Nile) and northern Egypt was Lower Egypt.

Just north of Cairo, the Nile fans out into a series of canals in an area known as the Delta. This area is still the most fertile part of Egypt, and was primarily used for agricultural land. During the New Kingdom there were numerous vineyards

The Nile at sunset, Luxor. (Photograph courtesy of BKB Photography)

here producing some of the finest grapes in Egypt. Unfortunately, due to the wetter soil in the Delta, archaeological remains are generally more fragmentary than those from other sites.

THE INUNDATION

The inhabited land along the Egyptian Nile has for the last 5,000 years covered an area of only 34,000 square kilometres. The fertility of the land was totally reliant on the annual inundation, as there was very little rain. In the Delta, for example, as the wettest part of the country, there may only have been 100–200 millimetres of rain a year. In order not to waste fertile land, houses, temples and settlements were built on the sand between the fertile soil and the cliffs that demarcated the start of the desert.

When it did rain in the south, it was considered important enough to record, and there are three pieces of New Kingdom graffiti from Deir el Medina referring to it. They all follow a single format: 'Year 4 of Baenra [Merenptah], first month of summer, day 27. This day the water of the sky came down.'

Due to the infrequency of rain the inundation was essential to Egyptian survival, and it dictated agricultural success and when monumental building works were carried out, as well as being incorporated into the religion and influencing the calendar, with New Year falling on the first day of the flood.

The Nile at Aswan started rising in June, increasing in volume until reaching its maximum height in September. This was a stressful yet welcomed time of year. If the inundation was too high the land would be ruined, and if it was too low the land would not be fertilised. Excessively high or low floods both resulted in failed crops and famine.

During the flood (July until October) farmers had little to do as their land was under water, and often they were conscripted to work on royal monuments. For

In an attempt to predict flood levels Nilometers were built along the Nile at major temples, such as Philae, Edfu, Esna, Kom Ombo and Denderah. These comprised a series of steps leading down to the water table. The level of the water was measured and records were kept of the highest levels. Measurements could then be compared to those of previous years in order to prepare for the coming flood.

Above: Victims of famine, from the causeway of Unas.

Below: Nilometer, Karnak Temple.

example, many manual labourers who built the Giza pyramids may have been corvée labourers. Contrary to popular belief, pyramid builders were not slaves, and excavations of the workers' village at Giza indicate that they were well fed, with beef, goat and sheep being regular dishes. There were enough meat bones discovered at the site to feed 6,000 people beef every day. Some were also given permission to build their tombs near the Great Pyramid, and from studying the bodies it is clear they were also given medical care while working at the site. When the Nile water started receding the farmers returned to their fields which were now covered in a thick layer of black, fertile silt. This led to Egypt being named Kemet, or Black Land. Since the High Dam at Aswan was constructed and opened in 1971, Egypt is no longer governed by these floods, as the water level remains consistent all year round.

Divisions of Egypt

The Egyptians liked to compartmentalise their world into duals and opposites in order to maintain cosmic equilibrium (Maat). For example, as Egypt was the Black Land, a fertile area of order; the desert, or the Red Land (Deshret), was the opposite, a desolate, chaotic place.

The Nile running through Egypt separated the country into east and west. The east was the land of the living, where the sun rose in the morning. The temples on the east bank were dedicated to living gods or cult deities. The west bank, on the other hand, was the place of the dead, where the sun set in the evening, and was the location of cemeteries. The temples here were dedicated to funerary gods and the deceased who had been deified. 'Residing in the West' was an often used euphemism for someone who had died.

Nomes

Other land division included the political regions known as nomes, which were rather like modern counties or boroughs. There were forty-two nomes in total, twenty-two in Upper Egypt and twenty in Lower Egypt. The boundaries of the nomes and the nome capitals changed over the centuries, although each nome was governed by a local mayor who answered to central government, reporting on taxation, crime, temple activities and financial matters. Each nome had a local council, as well as specific practices, gods and religious laws. All, however, were under the centralised control of the king.

UPPER AND LOWER EGYPT

The most important political division was that of Upper and Lower Egypt. Upper Egypt started at the Nile cataracts at Aswan, which acted as a natural defence for the southern border of Egypt. The city of Asyut is thought by some to be the dividing line, with everything south of here being Upper and everything north being Lower Egypt. However, no king could consider himself the king of Lower Egypt until he ruled Memphis, indicating the true division lay here.

This division was particularly important for the ideology of kingship, for to be a true king one had to rule a united Egypt. The politically unstable intermediate periods, which fell between the main Kingdoms (Old, Middle, New), were defined by kings who ruled either Upper or Lower Egypt; but not both. However, some kings of these periods called themselves king of Upper and Lower Egypt when they were not, in order to prove they were an ideal king.

The first unification of the 'Two Lands' was possibly carried out by King Narmer in Dynasty 0 (approximately 3100 BCE) and is recorded on the Narmer Palette in the Cairo Museum. This shows the first incident of the 'smiting pharaoh' scene, which is repeated by almost every king throughout the rest of Egyptian history. Narmer is

Above left: Sm3 tawy symbol, which appears on many royal statues. Colossi of Memnon, Luxor.

Above right: The Seth animal, Open Air Museum, Karnak Temple.

shown on one side of the palette wearing the white crown (*hedjet*) of Upper Egypt in this traditional smiting pose, arm raised and poised to hit a kneeling enemy with a mace. On the rear, the king is presented in procession wearing the red crown (*deshret*) of Lower Egypt, showing that he was now king of both Upper and Lower Egypt.

The importance of the unification of Egypt was incorporated into the five titles adopted by a new king. These titles include a carefully chosen name designed to reflect the king's nature, political aims or beliefs. The classical order was:

1. The Horus name. This name was written in a *serekh* frame, a rectangle representing the palace with the god Horus seated on top.
2. He of the two ladies name. These ladies were the vulture goddess Nekhbet, from el Kab in Upper Egypt, and the cobra goddess Wadjet, from Buto in Lower Egypt. These two goddesses can be seen on the crown as the double uraeus.
3. The Golden Horus name. Some believe the gold reference may be due to the Egyptians controlling the Nubian gold mines, or it could emphasise the divinity of the king as the living Horus. Gold was considered divine as it was eternal and never tarnished.
4. The Throne name (in a cartouche) and He of the sedge and the bee. This is the first of two names in a cartouche and was given to the king when he was crowned. The sedge and the bee represent Upper and Lower Egypt consecutively.
5. The birth name (in a cartouche) with Son of Ra. This was the name given to the king at birth and is often the name we are more familiar with. The Son of Ra title emphasised the divinity of the king, and his right to rule Egypt.

The king's jurisdiction is also identified by his crowns. There were three crowns associated with this essential role: the white crown of Upper Egypt, which is tall and conical, the red crown of Lower Egypt which is red and L-shaped and the double crown where the white is slipped inside the red crown and they are worn together. Often, the crown worn is dependent on location, so a temple in Upper Egypt will have the king wearing primarily the white or the double crown, and vice versa should the image be in Lower Egypt.

Right: The Son of Ra title of Thutmosis.

Below left: White crown of Upper Egypt, Deir el Bahri. (Photograph courtesy of BKB Photography)

Below right: Red crown of Lower Egypt, Deir el Bahri. (Photograph courtesy of BKB Photography)

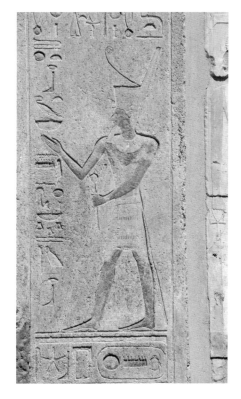

Prior to this, Egypt was divided into numerous areas with their own leaders and laws. Narmer possibly united these after a series of battles that necessitated laying siege to individual walled cities. This desire to unify the country may have developed from the need to utilise the Nile for survival and the necessary organisation of large numbers of people to build, maintain and protect earthworks. This type of work needed a centralised controller. It is easy to see how one leader could slowly take over a number of smaller communities, gaining enough power to control larger communities until they ruled a whole region, if not the whole country.

Since this initial unification, every king wanted to emulate Narmer in ruling a united Egypt. Many royal statues bear the sm3 tawy scene on the throne base, which represents the unification of the two lands. There are two figures, either two of the king, Horus and Seth, or two images of Hapy, the god of the Nile inundation, tying a papyrus stalk (Lower Egypt) and a lotus flower (Upper Egypt) around the heart and lungs of Egypt.

Horus and Seth represented the duality of order and chaos, as without one the other could not exist. Seth was the god of chaos and was represented with the head of an aardvark, with long, flat-topped ears, the body of a dog (when in animal form), and a forked tail, whereas Horus, the god of order, was represented as a falcon, or as a man with a falcon's head.

CAPITAL CITIES

As the country was divided into Upper and Lower Egypt, there were generally two capital cities, one in the north and one in the south, representing a religious and an administrative capital. Some kings expanded on established cities whereas others constructed a new capital city. Some cities, like Tell el Dab'a in the Delta, were chosen as the capital due to the extensive trade routes into Egypt, and the city was dominated by a harbour. Akhetaten (Tell el Amarna), on the other hand, was chosen by Akhenaten (1350–1334 BCE) because no other god had been worshipped there previously. Each king clearly had their own reasons for choosing their main residence.

PRE-DYNASTIC CITIES

During the pre-dynastic and early dynastic periods there were three major cities. Naqada (or Nubt) was the largest and was situated on the west bank approximately 26 kilometres north of Luxor. The city was considered important enough for royal burials and one of the *mastaba* tombs contained ivory labels and clay seals naming King Aha (*c.* 3050–2890 BCE). The tomb is thought to have belonged to his wife Neithhotep.

Hierakonpolis, another important site during this period, had extensive settlements and cemeteries that included the funerary temple of King Khasekhemwy (*c.* 2686 BCE). The earliest decorated tomb, Tomb 100, was also discovered here, but is now unfortunately lost. It may have belonged to one of the ruling chieftains of the area. Archaeologists also uncovered the earliest Egyptian temple, which was originally dedicated to Horus. His position in the Egyptian pantheon and his connections to kingship indicate this town was an important one.

Abydos was the third major pre-dynastic settlement, although it remained an important site for another 4,500 years. The majority of the pre-dynastic burials there are of the upper elite and royal family, including numerous funerary enclosures and twelve boat burials. These contained wooden hulls of boats 18–21 metres long and 50 centimetres high with a mud-brick structure encasing them. Boulder anchors had also been included. It is generally accepted that these boats

Boat of Khufu, Giza.

were created purely for the afterlife and formed part of the funerary entourage, or represented lunar, solar or stellar barques for the deceased to travel with the gods. The Abydos boats are the earliest association with the king, although the most famous funerary boat belongs to King Khufu (2589–2566 BCE) at Giza.

One of the largest Abydos tombs was Tomb U-j, which consisted of twelve rooms containing numerous funerary items including bone, ivory and pottery artefacts. There were also approximately 400 Palestinian jars, containing the remnants of wine, which was identified by the presence of grape pips, salt of tartaric acid, terebinth and stringed fig slices. At this time wine was not produced in Egypt, so these jars were obviously imported. Abydos contained monuments of all the first dynasty kings and two of the second dynasty kings, indicating that it was an important political centre.

OLD KINGDOM MEMPHIS

By the Old Kingdom, Memphis had taken over from these cities as the administrative centre and remained important throughout dynastic history, although now it is mostly lost under modern Cairo. The Old Kingdom temple of Ra at Heliopolis was bigger than the Karnak temple complex, and during the reign of Sety I and Ramses II, the harem and royal lodges were situated here, suggesting Memphis was still considered important. The cemeteries associated with this city, on the west bank, include the pyramid complexes of Giza, Saqqara, Dahshur, Abusir and Abu-Roash. Memphis remained the capital for such a long time because of its position on the Nile, with easy access routes and control over the Delta and the Nile Valley.

DELTA RESIDENCES

The Delta city Avaris (Tell el Dab'a) was the capital city during the Second Intermediate Period under the Hyksos rulers. Excavations here have uncovered a vast settlement dating from the earlier Middle Kingdom, with intact tombs, houses and temples. The nature of the settlement shows an interesting juxtaposition between two cultures, Egyptian and Palestinian (where the Hyksos originated). The most remarkable finds from this site are donkeys accompanying some elite burials and the eighteenth-dynasty Minoan frescos of acrobats and bulls leaping from what may have been a palace dated to the time of Thutmosis III (1504–1450 BCE).

The Giza Plateau.

This city maintained its importance throughout the New Kingdom and was extended during the reign of Ramses II to form the capital Pi-Ramesses (modern Tell el Dab'a-Qantir). Pi-Ramesses was initially built by Sety I as a harbour town, and controlled transportation of goods from the Mediterranean into the Nile Valley. Ramses II turned this major harbour town into the royal residence, and wanted it to rival the beauty of Memphis or Thebes. By the end of the twenty-second dynasty the local branch of the Nile had unfortunately dried up, leaving Pi-Ramesses cut off and resulting in its abandonment.

THEBES

Throughout the New Kingdom, Thebes (Luxor) was the religious capital of Egypt, home to the most important deity of the period, Amun. Thebes has produced more archaeological evidence than any other site. Not only did the city accommodate the famous temples of Karnak and Luxor, but the west bank also contains royal burials in the Valley of the Queens and that of the Kings, and the royal funerary temples. Situated on the west bank is the well-preserved settlement of Deir el Medina, the purpose-built village to accommodate the Valley of the Kings' workmen.

TELL EL AMARNA

The only time when Thebes was not the favoured religious capital during the New Kingdom was under Akhenaten. He decided to move the capital to Akhetaten (Tell el Amarna) in Middle Egypt, as the site had never been used to worship any other deity, which was ideal for his newly revered deity, the Aten. He chose this site in particular due to a dip in the surrounding cliffs within which the sun rose, resembling the hieroglyphic sign for sunrise.

Excavations at the site have uncovered temples, palaces, tombs, military barracks and houses. When Akhenaten died in year 17 of his reign, the city was quickly abandoned and everyone returned to Thebes.

TANIS

At the end of the New Kingdom the capital city moved again, returning to the Delta and the city of Tanis. The earliest building work here was carried out by Psusennes I (1039–991 BCE) of the twenty-second dynasty. Many of the blocks used to build Tanis were taken from the abandoned city of Pi-Ramesses. Temples at Tanis were dedicated to Amun, Mut, Khonsu and Astarte; they continued to be used until the Ptolemaic period. The tombs of the twenty-first and twenty-second dynasty kings were discovered here and contained silver coffins. The tombs were discovered in 1939, just as the Second World War started, and although they were intact upon discovery they were never given the publicity they deserved.

ALEXANDRIA

The capital city during the Ptolemaic period was Alexandria on the northern coast of Egypt, built by Alexander the Great in 332 BCE. The city was culturally Greek, and today this ancient city is under modern Alexandria. Fragments of the famous lighthouse of Pharos, one of the ancient wonders of the world, have been discovered in the Mediterranean just off the coast. Underwater excavations near the fort of Qait Bey covering an area of 2.5 hectares have recovered 2,500 blocks of pillars, column bases, capitals, sphinxes, statues and granite blocks probably from the lighthouse itself. The statues and sphinxes date from the Middle Kingdom through to the Ptolemaic period, indicating the Ptolemaic city was filled with remnants of Egypt's ancient past. It is fascinating to consider that when Cleopatra VII was on the throne (51–30 BCE), almost 3,000 years of pharaonic history had passed, and people then were possibly as fascinated with the life of the ancient Egyptians as we are today.

Fort of Qait Bey, Alexandria. The site of the Pharos lighthouse.

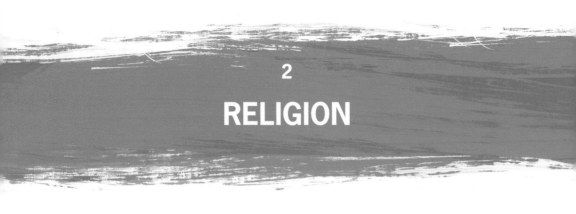

2

RELIGION

Fundamental to Egyptian culture was religion. There were hundreds of deities, many with animal heads, each having a specific role, imagery, mythology and cult practices. The anthropomorphic gods were believed to possess the characteristics associated with the animal represented, but there was no active worship of the animal itself. For example, Hathor, a cow-headed goddess, was worshipped as a mother goddess, as the cow was associated with milk and sustenance.

EGYPTIAN GODS

The pantheon was separated into state and personal deities. State religion was that of the king and is presented in temples throughout Egypt. These gods were

Hathor with a cow's head, Deir el Medina.

concerned with the complexities of environmental cycles (solar and flood), kingship succession, battles and cosmic equilibrium (Maat). Such concerns were too complex for ordinary people to comprehend as their worries included illness, fertility and childbirth. Therefore different deities were worshipped in the home that helped with such concerns.

There were of course some deities who appealed to both king and commoner: Isis for example, the mother of Horus and general mother goddess, or Ptah, a creator god worshipped at Deir el Medina as the god of craftsmen.

CREATION MYTHS

Religion was used in Egypt, as elsewhere, to explain environmental cycles and world formation, in the form of creation myths. Although the deities concerned were state gods, everyone was familiar with the stories. There were however, variants on the creation story, with different supreme deities dependening on time and location.

The primary myth concerns the Ennead of Heliopolis, the nine most important deities of the pantheon. According to this myth, creation took place in Heliopolis, just outside modern Cairo. In the time before creation the world was empty, except for darkness and primordial waters known as Nu or Nun. Although there was a sacred lake in every temple in Egypt reminiscent of this primordial water, there were no temples or shrines dedicated to Nun in his own right.

A small mound of earth arose from the primordial water, upon which a lotus flower emerged. From this flower the solar deity Atum came into existence. Such a mound was familiar to the ancient Egyptians, as it recalled the first visible land masses after the annual inundation started to abate. As a solar god, his self-creation saw the birth of the sun and the first dawn. Atum, although male, was able to self-reproduce through spilling bodily fluids. The next generation of gods, Shu and Tefnut, were created from spit and semen. Utterance 527 of the Pyramid Texts states, 'Taking his phallus in his grip and ejaculating through it to give birth to the twins Shu and Tefnut'. This makes it clear that Atum masturbated to create the next generation of gods. However, Utterance 600 claims they were born from his mouth.

Shu was the god of air, and his name means void or empty. He is depicted as a man with arms raised to support the sky, filling the space between the sky (Nut) and the earth (Geb). The Pyramid Texts (Utterance 222) state that the bones of Shu were the clouds used by the king to descend to heaven. Tefnut, his sister, whose name means 'to spit', was the goddess of moisture and was believed to be visible in the morning dew which purified the land.

Nut the sky goddess. Denderah temple.

Shu and Tefnut produced the next generation of gods, Geb and Nut. They formed the boundaries of the sphere that was the world containing Shu and Tefnut, with Nun the primeval water surrounding the exterior. The sun was unable to exist in the area outside this sphere. In the tomb of Ramses VI (1141–1133 BCE), the sun god is depicted travelling along Nut's body. It was swallowed at dusk, and travelled inside her body until its rebirth in the morning.

Nut and Geb's children were the most important gods in the pantheon: Osiris, Isis, Seth and Nephthys. The first five deities of the Ennead (Atum, Shu, Tefnut, Geb and Nut) explained the environment in a simplistic way, whereas the mythology of the final four deities explained the laws of kingship and succession.

ISIS AND OSIRIS MYTH

The Turin King List (dated to Ramses II, 1279–1212 BCE) records the time when Egypt was ruled by the gods – Ptah, followed by Ra (sun god), then Shu, Geb and Osiris. As king, Osiris taught the people how to farm, make wine, obey laws and believe in the gods. His wife, Isis, taught wives how to make bread and beer. Osiris's brother, Seth, was envious of Osiris's popularity and plotted against him in order to take the throne for himself. The most detailed version of this story comes from Plutarch's *Isis and Osiris* (120 CE), although there are fragments in the Old Kingdom Pyramid Texts.

Seth collected the measurements of Osiris and built a box of priceless wood to fit them exactly. At a banquet Seth announced that whoever could fit into the box could keep it. Many people tried but could not fit. Osiris then lay down in the box and fit perfectly. Seth closed the lid before casting the chest into the Nile where it floated away, drowning Osiris.

When Isis heard about this she immediately began searching for the chest. She learnt that a casket had been found in Byblos and travelled there to retrieve it. After some time, she located the chest and returned with it to Abydos. After unloading the chest she fell into a deep sleep, only to be discovered by Seth who was hunting crocodiles in the area. He recognised the casket and cut the body of Osiris into fourteen pieces and scattered them throughout Egypt. When Isis awoke she was distraught at the desecration of her husband's corpse. Her tears are believed to be the cause of the first inundation.

Isis and her sister Nephthys started to search for Osiris's body parts. They eventually found all the pieces except the penis, which had been eaten by a fish.

The Osirion in Abydos. A temple built on the site of the burial of Osiris's body parts.

Isis raises Osiris from the dead, Abydos. (Photograph courtesy of BKB Photography)

Wherever they discovered a part they built a tomb, the most important of which was Abydos, where the murder had taken place. In the later periods of dynastic history the murder was ritually re-enacted annually to ensure that the cycle of life continued. Abydos was an important place of pilgrimage for many Egyptians. If it was not possible to visit Abydos in life, a model boat was placed into the tomb so the journey could be made in the afterlife.

The final scene of this myth is recorded most fully at Sety I's chapel to Sokar at Abydos. Isis resurrected Osiris and turned herself into a kite, using her wings to breathe life back into him. She modelled a penis from clay and became impregnated with Horus. After that final act Osiris was banished to the realm of the dead, where he remained as the god of the Underworld. Seth then took over the throne of Egypt from his brother.

CONTENDINGS OF HORUS AND SETH

Horus was raised secretly by his mother Isis in the marshes until he was old enough to take his place on the throne. However, Seth still wanted to rule, and called for a tribunal held by the Ennead, which lasted eighty years. The Contendings of

Above left: Ra-Horakhti, Denderah. (Photograph courtesy of BKB Photography)

Above right: Sety I and Hathor as his divine mother, Abydos. (Photograph courtesy of BKB Photography)

Horus and Seth describes this tribunal and is recorded on the Chester Beatty I Papyrus (twentieth dynasty).

Ra-Horakhti (sun god) presided over the tribunal and supported Seth, whereas the other deities believed, as the son of Osiris, the throne rightfully belonged to Horus. There were various judgements, each declaring Horus to be the rightful king, but Seth refused to accept the decision.

He boasted that the throne was his by right on the basis of his personal strength, before challenging Horus to a battle, demanding they both turn into hippopotami, and submerge themselves in the water for three months. The one to re-emerge should be given the crown. After they submerged themselves Isis was distressed, and made a fishing line with a copper barb and cast it into the water, where it pierced first Horus and then Seth. Both appealed to her for mercy, the former as her son, the latter as her brother. Isis felt compassion and released them both. Horus was furious that she had shown mercy to Seth, and cut off her head, which was to be replaced with that of a cow meaning Isis and Hathor are sometimes interchangeable.

Ra-Horakhti ordered that Horus should be punished. Seth found him asleep under a tree, attacked him, plucked out his eyes and threw him down the mountain. Hathor discovered Horus weeping in the desert and healed him by milking a gazelle into his eyes. She reported his injuries to Ra-Horakhti and the Ennead, who demanded Horus and Seth stopped their arguing. Seth agreed and asked Horus to dine at his house that evening.

After the meal, when Horus was sleeping, Seth inserted his erect phallus between Horus's thighs. Horus caught the semen in his hand and showed Isis what Seth had done. Becoming angry, Isis cut off Horus's hands and threw them into the river, making new ones from clay. She then made Horus ejaculate into a pot. She poured the semen over Seth's lettuce garden and when Seth ate a lettuce the next day he became pregnant. Seth reported the incident to the Ennead.

Horus decided to settle the argument with a race in stone ships. Horus, however, built a boat of pine and covered it with gypsum to resemble stone. Seth sliced off the top of a mountain and fashioned a boat from it. They started their race in the presence of the Ennead. Seth's boat sank and he transformed himself into a hippopotamus and attacked Horus's ship; Horus aimed a copper harpoon at him but the Ennead stopped him. Horus later complained that he had been in the tribunal for eighty years and was constantly winning against Seth, but still was not king. After some deliberation and intervention by Osiris in the Underworld, the Ennead arrived at the conclusion that the throne of Egypt should belong to Horus. As a consolation Seth was to accompany the sun god on his solar barque to fight the enemy of the sun god, the snake Apophis.

This myth introduces a number of deities and confirms the act of succession as well as the balance of order (Horus) over chaos (Seth).

SUN WORSHIPPERS

In the myths discussed so far we have been introduced to two solar gods, Atum and Ra-Horakhti. The solar cult was the most important in Egypt and there were many forms of the sun god, the most important of which was Ra, who was prominent throughout most of Egyptian history. Numerous other cults solarised their gods by amalgamating them with Ra, introducing new deities such as Ra-Atum, or Amun-Ra.

In the New Kingdom, Amun-Ra became the most powerful of the deities and was closely associated with kingship. The king always adopted the title Son of Ra (see chapter 1), but appealed to Amun in times of battle and unrest. Amun was also invoked in New Kingdom divine birth scenes, which emphasised the divinity of a king and their right to rule by depicting Amun as their biological father.

BOOK OF THE CELESTIAL COW

Ra, in addition to being involved in myths of other deities, also featured in his own, known as the *Book of the Celestial Cow*, which records his withdrawal from mankind. The earliest copy was found on the outermost gilded shrine of Tutankhamun (1334–1325 BCE). The myth starts at sunrise, at the birth of the sun, who got older as the day progressed until in the late evening he is shown as an old man leaning on a stick (normally with a ram's head).

In the myth, mankind had lost respect for Ra and formed a rebellion. Ra's daughter Hathor, normally a peaceful goddess of protection, was sent to earth to bring mankind to order in her form of Sekhmet, the lioness-headed goddess. In this form she devoured and slaughtered mankind. Ra was distressed by what he saw and conspired to defeat her. Ra and his servants poured red ochre into beer and flooded the area where she was sleeping. When she woke she drank the beer, believing it to be blood, and she was rendered unconscious once more.

Although mankind was saved and their faith in Ra had been restored, he withdrew from ruling to begin his journey across the sky in his solar barque. This journey was dangerous, and Ra was protected by Nut, the sky goddess. Ra left Thoth in charge of mankind, and he rewarded them by teaching them how to write hieroglyphs, the words of the gods, as well as dividing the year into three seasons – inundation, ploughing and harvest – comprising a total of twelve months.

Nun commanded Nut to change herself into a cow so Ra could rest upon her back in his frailty. When the weight of the sun became too much, Shu was ordered to support the sky with his upraised arms. Mankind was surprised to see their king travelling on the back of a cow and they strove to protect him, shooting arrows at his enemies. Ra's withdrawal marked a separation between the realm of the gods and mankind.

This story explains the solar cycle with the sun's emergence on the eastern horizon and setting in the west, plunging mankind into darkness for twelve hours while he continued his journey through the underworld. Sunset was viewed as the death of the sun.

This cycle also led to the important *heb sed* ritual, where the king, like Ra, had to prove he was not too old to rule by performing a rejuvenation ceremony every

Above left: Sekhmet statue, Mut complex, Karnak.

Above right: Thoth, the god of writing. Temple of Montu, Karnak.

thirty years. He was required to run a number of times around six markers that were representative of the boundaries of Egypt. This race was at times run against a bull.

THE DUNG BEETLE

Although other solar deities did not appear in their own mythology, they were still important to the solar cycle. One of these was Khepri, the scarab or dung beetle, an image synonymous with Egypt. He represented the sun at dawn and was shown pushing the sun from the underworld starting the daytime journey across the sky.

This imagery evolved from the nature of the dung beetle, which rolls a ball of dung across the ground. It also lays eggs within the ball, and when they hatched it appeared to the Egyptians that the ball (i.e. the sun) was self-creating.

Right: Heb Sed of Sety I, Abydos. (Photograph courtesy of Richard Sellicks)

Below: Khepri, the beetle solar deity. Karnak temple. (Photograph courtesy of Wouter Hagens, Wikimedia Commons)

ATEN: THE SOLAR DISC

The Aten was particularly important during the reign of Akhenaten in the eighteenth dynasty, and represented the solar disc. The Aten was portrayed as a sun disc with a uraeus on the lower arc. Hands on the end of the sunrays emanating from the disc often held the symbol of life (the ankh), offering it to the mouth and nose of Akhenaten, his queen Nefertiti and their daughters.

Only Akhenaten and the royal family were allowed to worship the Aten and everyone else worshipped the royal family. The Aten does not appear in any myths and is androgynous, neither male nor female. It is constantly present above the heads of the people, and worship was carried out in the open air, temples having rows and rows of open-air offering tables. After Akhenaten's death the Aten returned to the role as a minor deity, leaving the pantheon open again for traditional deities.

PRIESTS

All of the temples within which this varied pantheon of gods were worshipped required staff. Priests were known as 'servants of the god'. The role of priest was generally not a vocational calling, as positions were given by the king or were hereditary titles. Some families held the same priestly title for numerous generations. Officially, the king named all priests in Egypt, as they acted on his behalf in the temples. However, in reality he only hired the high priests of the main temples at Memphis, Thebes and Heliopolis, leaving lower ranks for the vizier to manage. At times when it was politically advisable for the king to control the power of the priesthood he chose them all.

Prior to the New Kingdom priests were part-time, working for one month a season, totalling three months a year. The remainder of the year they returned to their primary job. It was expected that their daily occupation dictated the priestly role issued. For example, doctors worked as priests of Sekhmet, the goddess of epidemics; lawyers became priests of Maat, goddess of truth; and scribes became priests of Thoth, the god of writing. Most part-time priests were *wab* priests (the pure ones), the lowest level of the priesthood. They played a supporting role, which included carrying the sacred barque, cleaning and supervising temple painters and draftsmen.

Priests purified themselves twice daily and twice nightly in the sacred lake of the temple and Herodotus (fifth century BCE) records that in addition they shaved all their body hair every other day.

With the introduction of a permanent priesthood in the New Kingdom it was possible to have a temple career, and hierarchy became important. The most

Sacred lake, Medinet Habu.

The king makes offerings to Amun. A priest generally performed these tasks as a proxy king. Karnak.

important role was the high priest, who was a representative or proxy king performing the rituals on behalf of the king himself. The king is always presented on temple walls as making offerings to the deities, but he was unable to officiate over all the daily temple ceremonies. The representative was therefore essential.

Between the high priest and the *wab* priest there were a number of other roles. For example, in the Graeco-Roman period the *stolist* priests were responsible for dressing the divine statue in the temple, adorning it with jewellery, anointing it with perfume and looking after the ritual materials. In the Middle Kingdom the Priest of the Loincloth probably held a similar position. Priests of the House of Life were scribes and scholars and worked in the House of Life, an institution where all religious texts were written, restored and stored. It is reputed to have had knowledge of medicine, geography, geometry, astronomy and the history of kings. The lector priest was responsible for carrying the sacred book during rituals, reciting the prayers and being present during divine oracles. These priests were regarded in society as magicians, as they were aware of the content of many sacred writings.

Particularly important priests were funerary priests (or *sem* priests), who carried out the rites and rituals on the body before burial, prayer recitations, water sprinkling, lighting of incense and the Opening of the Mouth ceremony, all essential for rebirth into the afterlife. This position was traditionally filled by the king's heir, although from as early as the first dynasty there were professional *sem* priests. Accompanying these priests were the *ka* priests, responsible for maintaining the cult of the *ka* (spirit) after burial through the recitation of prayers and supplying offerings of food and drink for the deceased. When the *ka* priests stopped carrying out these rituals the deceased was no longer able to reside in the afterlife.

Priestesses

The roles of women in the temple were as varied as those of men and included such positions as singers, dancers and priestesses, although they were generally reserved for the cults of the goddesses, such as Hathor, Isis or Sekhmet. Singers and musicians were important, as prayers were probably sung, and they are often depicted holding the *menat* necklace or the sistrum, which were used to keep time. The *menat* necklace was made of beads and rattled when shook and the sistrum, sacred to Hathor, comprised a bronze arch through which short bronze sticks were threaded, mounted on a handle.

The title of God's Wife of Amun, introduced in the New Kingdom by King Ahmose (1570–1546 BCE), was the highest female title in the priesthood and was always held

Above: Goddess holding a *menat* necklace and a sistrum. Abydos. (Photograph courtesy of BKB Photography)

Right: God's Wife of Amun, Medinet Habu. (Photograph courtesy of BKB Photography)

by a royal woman. In the New Kingdom she was able to marry and have children, but in the unstable Third Intermediate Period the role became a celibate one in order to prevent any possibility of a royal takeover from this faction. The God's Wife lived at Karnak and was responsible for numerous rituals within the temple.

In later dynasties, power of the priests of Amun was transferred to the God's Wife and the women held more power than the priests. Many God's Wives had their own funerary chapels within the boundaries of the temple at Karnak and Medinet Habu; unheard of for male priests. The God's Wives are also shown performing rituals directly with the god Amun.

THE TEMPLE

Each temple also needed a number of auxiliary workers, including caretakers, janitors, workmen, bakers, butchers and florists. Although temples were bustling places, with many members of staff, they were not open to the public. Only the king, priests and a select few could enter the temple, and none but the king and high priest could enter the holy of holies where the statue of the god resided.

The entire temple and its rituals revolved around this sanctuary and the statue within, which was generally small (about 30 centimetres) made of gilded wood or gold. Twice daily this statue was removed from the sanctuary and washed, dressed in fresh linen and had make-up and perfume applied before being fed. The god took nourishment from the food, which was then distributed among the priests. It was believed that the *ka* of the god resided in the statue and took pleasure and nourishment from these rituals.

The same rituals were carried out in the homes of the Egyptians at their personal shrines by family members rather than priests.

PERSONAL RELIGION

Household gods reflected personal concerns, and many were associated with fertility, pregnancy and childbirth. Childbirth was one of the most dangerous times in a woman's life, with approximately 1.5 per cent of mothers dying, and infant mortality was as high as 50 per cent, so divine intervention at this time was essential.

Most houses had a shrine in the first room for small stela, statues and amulets, and this acted as the place of worship for the family. Twice a day, offerings of food and drink were made to these gods. The food could then be eaten after the gods had absorbed nourishment from it.

BES THE HAPPY DWARF

One of the most commonly represented household gods was Bes. From the eighteenth dynasty he was shown as an achondroplastic dwarf with a lion's head and tail. He is depicted facing forward with bowed legs, feet turned outwards, his arms bent at the elbows and his hands placed on his hips. His lion face is sometimes thought to be a mask, and a cartonnage mask was discovered at el Lahun together with items used in childbirth. It is thought to have belonged to a midwife, doctor or dancer. A similar mask of moulded clay was also discovered at Deir el Medina.

He is sometimes shown carrying the *sa* symbol of protection, a knife, or two snakes and a gazelle, indicating that he defeated evil. Bes appears on ivory wands used in birthing rituals holding a knife, which he used against harmful demons. He had many roles, including being the god of love, marriage, jollification, and the guardian of Horus the child – therefore protector of all children. Through the process of singing, dancing and music he chased away snakes, scorpions and all forces of evil or malevolent spirits.

Bes was closely associated with the goddess Taweret and they were often represented on the same objects such as furniture, headrests, pottery vessels, kohl tubes, cosmetic spoons and mirrors.

PTAH, THE ULTIMATE CRAFTSMAN

An important god for the workmen at the village of Deir el Medina was Ptah, the patron of artists, stonemasons and craftsmen. As a personal god he protected the creative industries, but he was also thought to cause blindness to those who did not uphold the laws of Maat. This was an ailment that frequently affected the workmen in the Valley of the Kings, as they worked in dark, dusty and confined spaces. As a state god his role was creator, creating the world as a craftsman works. He is often depicted in a divine triad with Sekhmet and their child Nefertum.

Above left: Bes, Denderah. (Photograph courtesy of BKB Photography)

Above right: Taweret, resting on the *sa* symbol, Edfu. (Photo courtesy of Karen Green, Wikimedia Commons)

TAWERET THE PREGNANT HIPPOPOTAMUS

Taweret was a pregnant hippopotamus, normally shown standing on her hind legs with pendulous breasts and a protruding stomach. She had the head of a hippopotamus, the four limbs and paws of a lion, and a mane in the form of a crocodile's tail. She was evoked during childbirth to scare away harmful demons and spirits.

As a fertility goddess, she was also associated with female sexuality and pregnancy and was affiliated with the goddess Hathor. She is hence sometimes shown wearing the cow-horn and sun-disc headdress common to Hathor.

Like Bes, Taweret carried the *sa* sign of protection, an ankh, a knife or a torch, the flame of which repelled evil spirits. In the funerary cult, Taweret was the Lady of Magical Protection, who guided the dead into the afterlife. Childbirth deities were often associated with rebirth, as the process was believed to be the same. With Hathor she protected the western mountains leading to the necropolis, consequently protecting the deceased at the start of their journey.

HATHOR

Another deity worshipped as a state and a personal deity was Hathor. In the home she was a goddess of sexuality and motherhood, and was a protector during childbirth. In the Book of the Dead she took the form of the Seven Hathors who pronounced the fate of the newborn baby. Her shrines were often approached by childless couples desperate to conceive who left votive offerings of clay or wooden penises, necklaces, beads or three-dimensional female figurines.

Within the villages Hathor was also worshipped as the Lady of Drunkenness, as it was believed that through drinking alcohol it was possible to experience the goddess and converse with her. The Festival of Drunkenness enabled the villagers of Deir el Medina to get drunk in the hope of communicating directly with the goddess. All festivals dedicated to Hathor involved playing instruments, especially the sistrum, singing and dancing.

Hathor also held a funerary function in her form as Lady of the West or Goddess of the Western Mountain. In these roles she protected the necropolis and all those in it. She is often depicted in this form as a cow emerging from the cliffs or overshadowing the tomb. As the Lady of the Sycamore, Hathor provided nourishment for the deceased in the form of a sycamore fig tree. She is depicted in this form in both royal and non-royal tombs.

ANCESTOR CULT

Each family also worshipped their own ancestors, who upon death and rebirth in the afterlife became Excellent Spirits of Re. These spirits were thought to be able to affect the life of the living and influence the gods of the afterlife. The ancestors worshipped were within two or three generations: parent, spouse, child or sibling. They were depicted on a small stela (approximately 25 centimetres in height) holding a lotus flower and standing before a deity, or seated and being worshipped by their living relatives.

These stela were often accompanied by ancestor busts consisting of small (less than 30 centimetres in height) human heads on a base. Some figures were bald and others had natural hair or large tripartite wigs. The only other adornment was a collar with lotus blossoms and buds hanging from it. Over 150 ancestor busts are known, mostly from Deir el Medina, but only five have hieroglyphic inscriptions, two with the title 'Housewife' and a name, and another with the name and titles of Hathor, suggesting the deity was portrayed in this instance.

The dead were very much part of everyday life in ancient Egypt and on special festivals, anniversaries or celebrations the families visited the ancestors in the tomb chapels for a meal. These feasts were sometimes served on pottery dishes inscribed with letters to the dead. People wrote asking for help in life or to recommend them to the gods. These letters were often written under stress, which is reflected in the handwriting and the unplanned nature of the requests.

As the ancestors that people worshipped changed as they slipped out of living memory, so did the wider pantheon of gods. New gods were created as community needs changed and old gods fell out of fashion. Deity worship and the associated rituals also varied from town to town and each town had its own religious cult and specific rituals. Egyptian religion was flexible, meeting the needs of the worshippers. Should there be a gap in this need a new god was created or an ancestor invoked who could address this need. Egyptian religion was therefore totally inclusive for all Egyptians. They could choose who they worshipped and how, and everyone from the poorest farmer to the king had their favourite who they worshipped above all others.

Lady of the Sycamore. Tomb of Thutmosis III, Valley of the Kings. (Photograph courtesy of The Yorck Project, Wikimedia Commons)

3
LIFE IN AN EGYPTIAN VILLAGE

Egyptian society was divided into a strict hierarchy, like a pyramid, with the king at the top, followed by a small number of officials, then the middle classes, and at the bottom the peasants. For the literate elite and middle classes there is a great deal of information about daily lives and religious beliefs. The information comes from a combination of archaeological evidence from the villages themselves and texts in the form of letters, literary tales, poetry and legal and administrative documents.

As less than 1 per cent of the population was literate, the picture we have of Egyptian daily life is limited to the middle classes and the elite. Unfortunately, for the majority of the population – the peasants – we have very little information.

Working in the fields, tomb of Khaemhat, Luxor. [Photograph courtesy of BKB Photography]

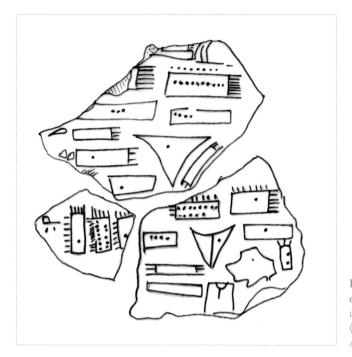

Laundry list from Deir el Medina. (Drawing after A. G. McDowell (1999) *Village Life in Ancient Egypt*, p. 61)

However, illiterate workers were still able to communicate in written form as is demonstrated by the New Kingdom laundry lists. The laundry men at Deir el Medina each collected clothes from approximately eight households daily to wash along the Nile edge. In order to record what they had collected, their laundry lists comprised drawings of the items (i.e. loincloths, fringed shawls and tunics), with a small dot marking how many of each had been collected.

In addition to written records, excavations of the villages themselves provide further information about architecture, living conditions and sanitation. There are a number of surviving village remains, including Deir el Medina, Tell el Amarna, el Lahun (Kahun) and Tell el Dab'a.

There are two types of village structure: the organic and the purpose built. Deir el Medina is an example of a purpose-built village, constructed to house the workmen who built the Valley of the Kings as a single project within a non-expandable village wall. Tell el Dab'a, however, was an organic town which was first inhabited in the Middle Kingdom and expanded until it was elevated to capital city during the Second Intermediate Period and again during the reign of Ramses II.

El Lahun (Kahun)

El Lahun was originally built to house the workmen who built the pyramid of Senusret II (1897–1878 BCE) in the Middle Kingdom, and is the largest known settlement from this period. It was originally called Hetep-Senusret and had an approximate ground area of 260 by 260 metres square. Initially it housed the workmen and their families; once the pyramid was complete it housed the priests who maintained Senusret II's funerary cult.

The village was surrounded by an enclosure wall and the streets and houses were laid out in regular lines and arranged so the western block, which was on higher ground, could be guarded by a single watchman. Evidence of channels in the streets between the houses to drain water from flash floods and to carry household waste were discovered by Petrie when he excavated. This is the earliest known drainage system of this type, and Petrie assumed all settlements had such systems.

To the west of the town was an elevated platform which Petrie called the Acropolis, or 'high city'. This platform accommodated a large palatial house which he thought may have housed the guards when the king visited. Others believe it to be an administrative centre, religious building or even the home of the mayor. There were also a number of large palatial buildings in the lower part of the town where it seems some of the highest officials in the land lived, which could have included the vizier, treasurer and the secretary of royal documents.

During the New Kingdom reign of Amenhotep III (1386–1349 BCE), el Lahun was re-inhabited, although only the western workmen's village was reoccupied, leaving many abandoned buildings. This occupation may have been in relation to the dismantling of the temple of Senusret II at el Lahun in order to reuse the blocks. People returned to the town in the Roman period, when the area was dug for limestone.

Deir el Medina

The village of Deir el Medina has provided most of the information we have about New Kingdom daily life. It was called 'The Place of Truth', and was built to house the workmen who carved and decorated the Valley of the Kings. It is situated on the west bank of the Nile at Luxor, away from Theban life. The inhabitants were dependent on the government for staples (food and water), and were extremely socially isolated. However, they were not prisoners, and moved freely to the markets on the east bank and relatives in other parts of the country.

The village now standing was initially constructed during the reign of Thutmose I (1524–1518 BCE), although most of the surviving evidence is from the nineteenth and twentieth dynasties when the village was at its prime. Although the village was built as a single project, over the centuries houses were extended, knocked through or remodelled, all within the non-expanding enclosure wall.

The village comprised approximately 120 houses, and only the tomb workmen and their families lived in the village itself. Auxiliary staff such as wood cutters, fishermen and gardeners lived outside the walls. The original village had one main street running north to south, with smaller narrow alleys running between the houses. These alleys may have been covered with reeds, providing shade from the sun. Each house had their own water jar, and records show their rations were 96–115 litres per day, per family. It is likely that water carriers delivered the water to a centralised water storage point and the families collected it from there. During the reigns of Ramses III (1182–1151 BCE) and later Ramses VI (1141–1133 BCE) they tried to dig a well, but were unsuccessful. The hole that remains is 52 metres deep, and when it was clear they were not going to reach water it was slowly filled up with rubbish and ostraca.

The cemetery was situated in the cliffs to the west of the village. These tombs are particularly interesting as they were constructed by the same men who cut and decorated the royal tombs, but there is less rigidity in the artwork, meaning scenes of daily life dominate over religious imagery.

The men of Deir el Medina all had a role to play in the construction of the royal tomb, so during the week all except the elderly and very young were absent from the village, working in the Valley of the Kings on the other side of mountain. The working week was ten days long, with nine days working and one day off. The workmen were divided into two gangs, the left side and the right side, although how this connected to their placement in the tomb is unknown. There was one foreman on each side, and like most occupations in Egypt it was hereditary, meaning it was common for one family to hold the position for generations. However, sometimes roles were filled by newcomers to the village. Conversely, there were often more children than jobs, and only one son could take the role of his father. The other sons no doubt left the village to gain employment elsewhere.

The village scribe was the same level as the foreman and was responsible for tomb administration – recording absences from work, number of tools distributed (and returned) and general work progression, which was passed to the vizier and ultimately to the king. This role was also hereditary. The scribe and the foreman were the highest-paid positions in the village. With no monetary system in Egypt,

Deir el Medina.

The attempt at digging
a well by Ramses III
and Ramses VI, Deir el
Medina.

The Valley of the Kings,
Luxor.

wages were in the form of rations, which included fish, vegetables, water, wood for fuel, pottery for household use and sometimes clothing. On festival days the workmen received extra rations, including sesame oil, blocks of salt, natron (a natural salt from the Wadi Natron) and even oxen.

Rations provided enough food to feed a large family plus a little extra to use as currency. Marketplaces worked on a barter system where items of clothes, food, animals, shoes and beer were swapped for other items. Each item had a relative market value, but this varied depending on demand. As long as the seller and the buyer were happy with the exchange it did not matter if the items were not of equal market value. However, there were still arguments about price. One document records how Mery-Re the carpenter made two statues for Ruty. On seeing the statues Ruty realised they were worth less than he paid. As they were unable to agree, they went to the oracle to solve the problem. The oracle sided with Ruty and Mery-Re was asked to reimburse him the difference in value.

Payday was on the twenty-eighth day of each month, but in year 29 of Ramses III these payments were delayed by six months, resulting in the workmen striking, with protests before the mortuary temples of Thutmosis III, Ramses II and Sety I, which were used as grain stores from which their rations were distributed. On this occasion the workmen received only half payment, because, in the words of the vizier, 'There is nothing left in the granaries. However, I shall give to you what is found there.' Later that same year the scribe Djhutymose went with two bailiffs to collect the grain himself from local farmers and temples as the rations had once again not arrived.

Deir el Medina was abandoned as a village at the end of the twenty-first dynasty, primarily because of security concerns of attacks by Libyans from the western desert. The villagers left Deir el Medina for the security of the temple complex at Medinet Habu. The village houses were then only used for storage.

AMARNA

The eighteenth-dynasty city of Tell el Amarna, or Akhetaten as it was known, was built during the reign of Akhenaten (1350–1334 BCE). Akhenaten decided he wanted a new city to dedicate to his favoured god, the Aten, on a site that had not been used previously to worship any other deity. This city, although built as one project, is different from Deir el Medina or el Lahun, as the palace forms the centre of the main settlement. This centre also included temples and military barracks, but no evidence has been found for shops, taverns or schools, so these activities may have taken place within the homes or open spaces. The houses expanded to the

Rat trap from El Lahun (UC16773). (Copyright Petrie Museum of Egyptian Archaeology, University College London)

north and south from this centre, each forming a small village-like area centred on a large official house. The cemetery was built on the periphery of the town.

The city was divided into quarters or suburbs, and communal wells were placed in public squares or were shared between several houses. There was also a sculptor's quarter and a workman village similar to Deir el Medina with seventy to eighty houses placed to the east of the city in the desert. Between 50,000 and 100,000 people lived at Tell el Amarna during the height of Akhenaten's reign, 10 per cent of whom were elite. The wealth of the homeowners was reflected in size and grandeur of the houses.

The workmen's village at Tell el Amarna was cramped, and evidence of rats, fleas and bed bugs has been found. Such living conditions become a breeding ground for tuberculosis and parasitic infections. It is thought fleas travelling on the Nile rat were responsible for the European bubonic plague, and evidence suggests that near the end of the reign of Akhenaten Amarna suffered an epidemic, killing many members of the royal family in a short space of time. Rats, however, were not just a problem at Amarna, as at the village of el Lahun Petrie discovered the earliest rat trap. It comprises a pottery box with slits in the side and a slidable end that can be raised in order to allow the rat to enter and lowered to prevent it escaping. Petrie commented that 'nearly every room has its corners tunnelled by the rats, and the holes are stuffed up with stones and rubbish to keep them back'.

There is evidence that pigs were kept in the workmen's village at Tell el Amarna. It is often stated the Egyptians did not eat pork, but they may have kept pigs as waste disposal. Evidence of parasitic worms contracted through eating undercooked and infected pork in mummies indicates, however, that pork was eaten.

This grandiose city was short-lived, and was quickly abandoned following Akhenaten's death. Tutankhamun (1334–1325 BCE) returned the capital city to Thebes, and the majority of people left Amarna. Only a couple of faience factories were still in use, but by the reign of Horemheb (1321–1293 BCE) these were also abandoned.

EGYPTIAN HOUSES

Although there were variations between settlements, the house layout and size was rather standardised. The houses at Deir el Medina were very similar to workmen's houses at other villages. They were only one storey, with a staircase at the rear leading to a flat roof which was used for storage and as a sleeping area, although one of the houses at Amarna has evidence of a small oven on the roof instead of the ground floor. Poorer families used the roofs more often than richer families, who had more square metres of space within the house itself. Many of the houses also had cellars, which were used for storage, and in some instances children were buried in these cellars or under the floors.

The houses were constructed of mud brick upon stone foundations. Mud bricks were made by mixing Nile mud with water and pouring it into brick moulds, which were left in the sun to dry. This method is still used in Egypt today. The outside of the house was whitewashed and the front door painted red. The wooden door frames bore the name of the inhabitants written in red ink, identifying who lived there in the absence of street names. This did not prevent letters and notes from going astray, and one villager tries to defend himself against the accusations of a woman by claiming he never received her note: 'As for the matters of illness about which you write me, what have I done against you? As for the medication which you mentioned, did you write me about them, and did I fail to give them to you? As Ptah endures, and as Thoth endures, I have not heard from anyone: It was not told to me.'

The majority of small houses had four rooms, the first opening on to the street. In this room there was an enclosed box bed, sometimes decorated with images of Bes and Taweret; in Amarna they were used as shrines to these deities. Some believe they may have been used for the birth of children, or even as a marital bed, and many clay models of women emphasising fertility were discovered in the structures.

Bernard Bruyère, who excavated at Deir el Medina (1922–1951), believes the box beds and figurines emphasised the important cult of the family in the home. Indeed the shrine housing statues of deities and ancestors was also located in this room.

The second room led off the first and was dominated by a large platform used as a seating area during the day and a bed at night. A false door stela dedicated to a favourite deity or ancestor allowed ancestral spirits to enter the house and participate in daily activities. Leading from this room was the third room, which served as a work area, storeroom and sleeping area for female members of the household. Often craftsmen used this room to work on private commissions which they sold to increase their household income.

The kitchen was at the rear of the house in a walled but open area with a clay oven and occasionally a silo for storing grain. Although the kitchen was outside, beams in the Amarnan houses were black with smoke from lamps, indicating poor ventilation, which led to a condition called anthracosis where soot settles in the lungs.

Although workmen's houses were compact, with some of the smallest houses at el Lahun measuring only 40 square metres, there were perhaps three generations living in them. Families on average had ten children, and unmarried female relatives may have resided in the family home. In addition to the human inhabitants, many households had cats for rodent control, a guard or hunting

A large house at Tell el Amarna.

dog, some ducks or geese (for eggs and later, meat) and goats (for milk). Early evidence at Deir el Medina shows cattle also lived within the village enclosure wall. Even in the large palatial houses at el Lahun, enclosed areas and feeding troughs indicate that livestock was housed near the large central courtyard. Rich houses no doubt smelt as bad as the poorer houses.

Other villages with a wider cross-section of society than Deir el Medina also had large palatial houses. These were often north facing to take advantage of the cooling northern winds. However, if this was not possible, a corridor led from the less-than-ideal entrance to a second, north-facing entrance. These houses were often complicated with numerous rooms and corridors. The house of Nakht, the overseer of public works at Amarna, for example, had thirty rooms, a large, columned reception hall, and a garden with an offering table to make open-air offerings to the Aten. Columns were a sign of wealth, and villas at Amarna and el Lahun had large, columned rooms designed to impress. Even in small workmen's houses they often had a wooden column in the first room painted to look like stone.

The main difference between a worker's house and an elite villa at Amarna were specific rooms designated as bedrooms, some with en-suite bathrooms. In Deir el Medina the living spaces were used as sleeping spaces at night, and people washed in the Nile or with a bowl of water. Large houses had purpose-built beds, whereas smaller homes used bed rolls for sleeping. Most people used headrests in place of pillows or cushions, made of wood, stone or clay. These were often decorated with images of Bes and Taweret, who protected them throughout the night.

Villas sometimes had en-suite stone-lined shower rooms, with a stone slab where the bather stood as a servant poured water over him. The water drained away through stone channels. Nakht's house also had a separate WC with whitewashed walls, one of which contained the earliest lavatory stool, a U-shaped wooden seat beneath which a bowl filled with sand was placed. Those not lucky enough to have an inside lavatory went outside. This no doubt led to a number of flies around the villages, resulting in, among other conditions, numerous eye diseases.

The Egyptians' reputation for wearing eye makeup derives from this problem, as thick eye makeup made of kohl, malachite, stibnite or galena had medicinal as well as aesthetic properties. Malachite is mentioned in the medical papyri, to be applied to eye infections or added to dressings for wounds. Although some eye infections were very serious and led to blindness, the only treatment was honey, ochre and galena. It was believed that blindness was caused by a deity whom the sufferer had offended.

Above left: False door, Karnak Temple. (Photograph courtesy of BKB Photography)

Above right: A shower at the palace of Ramses III at Medinet Habu.

Many houses, regardless of size, had a door keeper's room, ensuring all visitors were vetted and announced. In the smaller houses it is likely that a child or elder sat here rather than a paid member of staff. Door bolts and keys have been found at el Lahun, suggesting it was possible to lock your home, but security was still clearly a concern. A letter from a woman at Deir el Medina requests her friend house sit while she is away: 'Please have Amenemwia stay in my house so he can watch it.'

Large houses were divided into suites, often consisting of small three-roomed apartments with a reception room, bedroom and side room, perhaps used as a dressing room or storeroom. These suites housed the women, guests and administrative staff. All these suites were centred on an open court with a southern covered colonnade. It is possible these courtyards may also have had trees or a central pool for bathing which may have contained fish and ducks. Some New Kingdom tomb images show the tomb owner seated by one of these pools with a small fishing rod.

DAILY DIET

As houses varied according to status and wealth so did diet. From archaeological, written and artistic evidence it is possible to identify the food available, although it is impossible to ascertain what recipes and proportions of ingredients were used.

The staple food of the Egyptian diet was bread made from emmer wheat or barley. There were different shaped loaves indicating different ingredients. For example, sticky fruit bread, shown in the Dokki Agricultural Museum, Cairo, was made with mashed dates between two layers of dough. Other loaves were rolled in cumin seeds and often the dough was enriched with fat, milk, and eggs.

ALCOHOL

The other main staple was beer, made from the previous day's stale bread, or partially cooked fresh bread. The water in Egypt was unsafe to drink, so weak beer was drunk by everyone, including children. The beer was thicker and more nourishing than modern beer and needed to be strained through a sieve before consuming. It was often flavoured with fruit, primarily dates.

Wine was also popular in ancient Egypt. Egyptian wine was best drunk young, only a year or two after the grape harvest. Studies carried out on six of the twenty-six wine jars from Tutankhamun's tomb by a Spanish team in 2006 showed all of them contained tartaric acid, a chemical produced by grapes, but one jar contained syringic acid, suggesting the wine was white. This was unusual, as white wine is not recorded in Egypt until the third century AD. This indicates this was a special jar.

There were different qualities of wine – wine for offerings, wine for taxes, wine for merrymaking, and a very popular heated wine called *shedeh*, made from pomegranates and grapes flavoured with spices. A label on a jar from the Malkata vineyard claims the wine within was 'blended', indicating they were mixing different grapes together to produce different flavoured wines.

With such alcohol consumption, Egyptians were known to get drunk, and in year 40 of Ramses III, the absentee record from Deir el Medina shows a man called Pendua took a day off work because he was drinking with Khons, and Iyerniutef simply said he was 'drinking' and could not attend work on the royal tomb that day.

One notorious Deir el Medina inhabitant, Paneb, was accused of behaving badly when drunk, falling into rages and threatening to kill not only his adopted father, Neferhotep, but also the foreman Hay. On another occasion Sety II's mummy had just been placed in the sarcophagus and Paneb, drunk, climbed atop it. A shocking action, as the king was considered to be a god incarnate. The Instruction of Ani (twenty-first or twenty-second dynasty) warns against such behaviour: 'Don't take to drinking, because if you speak, something else [other that what you meant] will come out of your mouth. You won't know what you are saying.'

MEAT

The majority of people ate very little meat, surviving on vegetables and fish. Those fortunate enough to eat fowl enjoyed wildfowl, duck, geese, pigeon, egret and squab, all of which were roasted. Beef was eaten rarely by anyone other than the elite. However, when it was eaten, every part of the animal was used: the blood was made into a type of black pudding, the offal was dried and the bones were boiled up for stock and soups. Ox heads were often depicted on offering tables, indicating this was the best cut of meat – in fact, suitable for a god.

Evidence from mummies, including those of Ramses II and his son Merenptah, indicates the wealthy ate too much meat and animal fat – the mummies show signs of arteriosclerosis, or a hardening of the arteries common with a high cholesterol level. Other causes are, however, suggested for this ailment. Many people suffered from parasitic worms and other infections (see chapter 5), which could exacerbate arteriosclerosis, and smoke inhalation from hearths and incense would have created a similar bodily reaction to smoking in the modern world.

Butchery for divine offerings, Medinet Habu. (Photograph courtesy of BKB Photography)

For the majority of people, vegetables and pulses formed the basis of their diet, including lettuce, lentils and chickpeas (called hawk-face due to their shape), hummus and *ful nabed* (broad bean), *ful madames*, and *tirmis*. Onions, which were smaller and sweeter than today, were eaten like apples, and food was garnished with garlic, radishes, leeks, cabbages, cucumbers, and celery. An image from Amarna shows a man eating his packed lunch which comprised bread, cucumber and an onion, all washed down with beer. Evidence from el Lahun indicates many of the houses had a small garden in which to grow beans, peas and cucumbers.

The Egyptians ate a great deal of fruit, which was used as a sweetener in food, wine and beer. The fruit included watermelons, pomegranates, raisins, figs and dates. Although mandrake fruits are toxic it is thought they were used as a narcotic at parties, and are often shown being held to the nose of revellers. Excavations at el Lahun and Deir el Medina show the Egyptians also had carob from the powdered pods of St John's Locust, often used now as a chocolate substitute.

A drummer at the Opet Festival, Luxor Temple.

ENTERTAINMENT

Food played an important role in the lives of the elite in the form of banquets. These are regularly portrayed in non-royal tombs, showing numerous guests, often segregated by sex. Married couples, however, were depicted sitting side by side. It is unknown whether the segregated sexes were in separate rooms or sitting opposite each other. Servants made sure the wine and beer flowed freely and tables were piled high with food. Many people no doubt overindulged, and in one tomb the servant said to a lady, 'Drink this, my lady, and get drunk,' to which the lady replied 'I shall love to be drunk!' Not surprisingly some scenes show women and men vomiting into vessels held by servants.

Musicians, either men or women, entertained the guests. There was often a lutist, a flute player, a blind harper, and a couple of girls keeping time with drums or by clapping. There were also dancers and acrobats, who were primarily women, wearing little more than a belt made of shells and a large weighted wig which swung as they moved. Banquets were held for a variety of reasons including funerals, religious ceremonies and general celebrations.

Other food-related pastimes were hunting, fishing and fowling, providing sport for the elite. The Fayoum (near el Lahun) was a popular place to catch birds in the marshlands using throw-sticks, or to fish in the lake with spears. Those who craved more excitement hunted in the desert for lion, gazelle, wild ox, wild sheep, jackal, wolf, hare, fox, hyena and ostrich. Anything they caught was eaten and the skin, fur or feathers used.

BOARD GAMES

When the Egyptians were not feasting they were big fans of board games, and perhaps even gambling. There are at least three popular board games from archaeological records: Senet, Mekhen and Hounds and Jackals. Everyone could play these games, either with a purpose-made board or by scratching a make-shift board into the sand using pebbles as pieces. Sadly there are no surviving rules for any of them.

The Egyptians did not have dice, using throw-sticks or knuckle bones instead. Throw-sticks had one dark and one light side, and knuckle bones, often from a sheep, had four distinct faces (flat, concave, convex and twisted). The combination of each side thrown determined how many spaces could be moved.

Mekhen, or the coiled snake game, is the oldest game, and was popular in the pre-dynastic period (pre-3100 BCE) and the Old Kingdom (2686–2184 BCE).

The board is constructed of concentric circles representing the coils of a snake, and the Pyramid Texts describe how the deceased should travel around the board from the tail to the head. There are slots along the body of the snake where the gaming pieces were placed, although the number was not standardised, nor was there a standardised direction, as the snakes coil both clockwise and anti-clockwise.

In the First Intermediate Period the game of choice was Hounds and Jackals. The board consisted of a box or block of wood with sixty small holes drilled into it, twenty-nine for each player and a large central hole which both players shared. Into these the pieces were placed – Howard Carter believed these pieces to be hairpins due to their shape. There are five pieces each, five with a dog's head and five with a jackal's head.

The most popular game was Senet, a game played on thirty squares and thought to be similar to backgammon. The game was known before the first dynasty (2686–2613 BCE) and continued in popularity throughout the dynastic period. It was a game of strategy, played by two players with seven or five dancers or gaming pieces. There were two different styles (cones and reels), making it easy to identify each player's pieces. The objective of the game was to move all the dancers through the thirty squares to the end. Some of the squares were marked with a hieroglyph, indicating a lucky or unlucky square, and there was likely some penalty or reward for landing on them.

By the New Kingdom the game had also taken on spiritual meaning and is represented in tombs with the deceased playing an unseen opponent. If they won, the deceased continued into the afterlife. This scene is used to represent Chapter 17 of the Book of the Dead, and a Senet board was an essential part of the funerary assemblage.

Life in an Egyptian village was a vibrant and bustling one, with the women preparing food and beer for the daily consumption of the family, children running around playing, and animals causing havoc in the homes. Such close living quarters were unsanitary and dangerous for the health, even with the introduction of drainage systems. However, this did not prevent the inhabitants of the village from enjoying a game of Senet and a chat with their friends over a couple of beers at the end of the day.

4
GROWING UP IN ANCIENT EGYPT

Childhood in ancient Egypt was not much different to childhood today, albeit somewhat shorter, with adulthood starting for both boys and girls in the early teens.

With the men working in the tombs, temples or fields throughout the week, it was the mother's responsibility to care for the children. Tomb images show women carrying babies in slings across their backs, keeping the babies close to the body while enabling the women to do their chores. Mothers therefore held a very special place in the heart of ancient Egyptians, and the Instruction of Ani emphasises this bond:

> Double the food your mother gave you,
> Support her as she supported you;
> She had a heavy load in you
> When you were born after your months,
> She was yet yoked to you
> Her breast in your mouth for three years
> As you grew and your excrement disgusted,
> She was not disgusted, saying 'What shall I do?'
> When she sent you to school
> And you were taught to write
> She kept watch over you daily
> With bread and beer in her house.

From this it is clear that mothers were responsible for all aspects of raising children, from breastfeeding to organising education and protecting the children from harm.

Children played an important role in the household and participated in the same activities as their parents, enabling them to learn their expected roles in

A young child shown naked.
A mastaba tomb, Giza.

life. In tomb art they are differentiated from adults by their size and their side lock of youth, which was a curled or plaited lock of hair on an otherwise shaved head. Children were also depicted as naked, although child-sized tunics have been discovered indicating that they did wear clothes.

At home, girls helped their mother cook, clean and take care of the children. As some women worked their daughters trained alongside them, and a perfect example is funerals, where the women were accompanied by their daughters dressed as miniature adults. The boys, once old enough, helped their father, so the activities varied depending on their father's occupation. One young boy described in a New Kingdom school book worked with a baker. His role was to prevent the baker from falling headfirst into the bread oven by holding his feet as he placed the bread on the fire.

Despite having such responsibilities at a young age, children were still children, and an image from the tomb of Neferhotep (TT49) shows a nanny looking after a boy and girl. She was taking at drink from a jar, oblivious to the door keeper waving a stick at the children as they passed. One wonders how the children had antagonised him.

SCHOOL

Although literacy was low in ancient Egypt, school was important for certain careers. The earliest reference to a school or house of instruction is from the Middle Kingdom and it is only from the New Kingdom that school texts and student tablets give an insight into how the school system worked.

For middle-class and elite boys who were expected to enter into government administration or the upper levels of priesthood, a school education was necessary. As women were unable to hold administrative positions, girls were not schooled in an official way. This is not to say that women were uneducated. From Deir el Medina there is evidence of literate women, and in some New Kingdom tomb images, scribal equipment is depicted under the chairs of the women rather than their husbands. They were obviously educated at home by their parents rather than partaking in the system offered to the boys.

There were a number of official scribal schools during the New Kingdom, situated at the Mut complex and the Amun temple at Karnak, the Ramesseum, Deir el Medina, Memphis and Sais. These official schools were primarily for the children of the upper elite, although lower-class boys could be admitted. The Theban schools trained boys for careers in central government, whereas other schools specialised in the priesthood, medicine or the army.

Boys not fortunate enough to be admitted to one of these institutions were educated by their fathers or were adopted by a local scribe in order to inherit the position after him. Although the young students were given the title 'son' or 'staff of old age' they were adopted as an apprentice rather than as a son.

Boys started their education at five years old, and were beaten regularly, as it was believed that 'a boy's ear is on his back; he hears when he is beaten'. In the *Miscellanies* (a collective book of teaching materials), a pupil praised his teacher for such methods: 'You smote my back and so your teaching entered my ear.'

Children were taught reading, writing and arithmetic. The writing material used in school was limited, consisting of ostraca (limestone or pottery sherds), a gesso-coated wooden or stone tablet which could be wiped clean after use, and a reed pen. For arithmetic a wooden counting stick made from an old piece of furniture was discovered at el Lahun, used to teach children to count up to 100. Reading was an exercise to be spoken aloud, but arithmetic was a silent subject, as the *Miscellanies* explains: 'On another happy occasion you grasp the meaning of a papyrus roll … you begin to read a book, you quickly make calculations. Let no sound of your mouth be heard; write with your hand, read with your mouth. Ask from those who know more than you, and don't be weary.'

Pupils were taught to write hieratic phrases before progressing on to famous Middle Kingdom texts. These were in an archaic form of the language, almost indecipherable to New Kingdom children. These texts included model letters which helped to improve writing, spelling, ability and accuracy. These texts consisted of advice for moral behaviour, and it was hoped the students would learn from them. Their studies therefore had an emphasis on honesty, humility, self-control, good manners and a respect for parents.

Texts were chanted aloud and a *Miscellanies* text indicates they were accompanied by instruments: 'You have been taught to sing to the reed pipe, to chant to the flute, to recite to the lyre.'

Once they had learnt the texts they wrote them down on gesso-coated wooden or stone tablets. It is often thought they wrote from dictation, but the mistakes are rarely a result of mishearing. Once the student mastered the hieratic script in this manner, he then progressed to the more difficult hieroglyphic script.

At approximately nine years old the child, if a talented scribe, considered pursuing a career in the temple, central government or military. They then entered an apprenticeship to train on the job in preparation for taking the role at the death of their father or mentor. This apprenticeship lasted for ten or twelve years depending on the complexity of the role or their personal ability.

At this important time of their life *The Satire of the Trades* (nineteenth dynasty) encouraged the child to choose the role of a scribe over all others: 'The greatest of all callings, there's none like it in the land. Barely grown, still a child, he is greeted, sent on errands, hardly returned he wears a gown. I never saw a sculptor as envoy, nor is the goldsmith ever sent.' This description makes it clear that even a young scribal apprentice received wealth and respect and was sent on errands others were not to be trusted with.

Many young boys preferred the idea of a soldier's life of victory and glory, but Papyrus Anastasi III, written during the reign of Sety II (1199–1193 BCE), explains the hardships of the army to a potential recruit, Inena:

What is it that you say they relate, that the soldier's is more pleasant than the scribe's profession? Come let me tell you the condition of the soldier; that much exerted one. He is brought while a child to be confined in the camp. A searing beating is given to his body, a wound inflicted on his eye and a splitting blow to his brow. He is laid down and beaten like papyrus. He is struck with torments.

Come, let me relate to you his journey to Khor (region of Palestine and Syria) and his marching upon the hills. His rations and water are upon his shoulder like the load of an ass. His neck has become calloused, like that of an ass. The vertebrae of his back are broken. He drinks foul water and halts to stand guard. When he reaches the enemy he is like a pinioned bird, with no strength in his limbs. If he succeeds in returning to Egypt, he is like a stick which the woodworm has devoured. He is sick, prostration overtakes him. He is brought back upon an ass, his clothes taken away by theft, his henchmen fled … turn back from the saying that the soldier's is more pleasant than the scribe's profession.

As intended, Inena decided to become a scribe instead of a soldier.

Archaeologically, no school buildings have been identified from the dynastic period, so it is unknown whether there was a designated place or if classes took place in private homes or public areas. We also do not know how many students were in a class at any one time but from *The Satire of the Trades* we know school either broke for lunch or stopped at lunch time, as the text warns the boys to use their afternoon wisely.

GAMES AND TOYS

As children helped with household chores or on the farm from a very early age there was limited time to enjoy games or play with toys, but that is not to say they did not indulge when they were able. El Lahun has been a great source of children's toys, especially clay examples made by the children themselves. These clay models were of hippopotami, pigs, crocodiles, an ape with beads inserted for eyes and a boat with two seats, one of which was pierced for a mast and has the remains of a rudder. The hippopotami toys were the most popular, although it is clear that some children were more talented with modelling clay than others.

More complex figures can be seen in the British Museum in the form of a cat and a mouse with a moveable jaw, or in the Cairo Museum in the form of ivory dancing dwarfs. These dwarfs were attached to a wooden block with lengths of

Linen doll, El Lahun (UC40580). (Copyright
Petrie Museum of Egyptian Archaeology,
University College London)

cord, which, when pulled, made them dance. As this is of such high quality it is possible it was not intended as a toy.

A number of jointed dolls were discovered in a house at el Lahun, which Petrie named 'the doll factory', although some of them were decorated with small lines of tattoos, indicating they were fertility figurines. The Petrie Museum has two rag dolls from el Lahun, both made from linen. Neither doll has removable clothing, and they have very limited detailing, indicating that they were real toys.

Both sexes liked to play ball games, and a number of wooden and leather balls have been found. One is made of six leather strips sewn together and stuffed with dried grass or barley husks. This was so well played with that it had been repaired in the past. There are tomb scenes showing girls juggling with such balls, as well as one showing a game of catch played while riding on the back of another child. An Old Kingdom child at Naqada was buried with a skittle set comprising nine calcite and breccia skittles and four porphyry balls.

Children also played a number of games outside, including a version of 'piggy' that involved wooden tip-cats of approximately 16 centimetres, which were thrown into the air. The child who hit the tip-cat the furthest with a stick before it hit the ground was the winner.

Other games did not require equipment and therefore could be played by all. One such game was the Donkey Game. An Old Kingdom tomb scene shows an older boy on all fours carrying two younger children on each side like saddle bags. The young children had to hold on to each other to remain on board. Another fun outdoors game was 'Erecting the wine arbour', in which two boys stood in the middle holding on to two or four other children (girls or boys). They spun them around as they leant back on their heels. This is one of the few games which were played by both sexes together.

A particularly interesting game that some Egyptologists believe is also a rite of passage is the Hut Game, where four young boys stood inside a hut or arbour. Two stood with their right hand in the air, and another pinned the fourth boy to the floor. This boy reaches his hand out of the enclosure to a fifth boy who was leaning down towards him. The caption above indicates he needs to escape by himself. This game is represented in a number of tombs and only ever involves boys. The second aspect of this game involved what appears to be a ritual dance around a fertility figure, showing there were deeper levels to the game.

TRANSITION TO ADULTHOOD

As children behaved like children, so did teenagers, and in one New Kingdom text a teacher tries to encourage his students to be more restrained:

> When I was of your age, I spent my time in the stocks
> It was they that tamed my limbs.
> They stayed with me three months
> I was imprisoned in the temple,
> Whilst my parents were in the fields
> And my brothers and sisters as well

The stocks he refers to were wooden blocks around the ankles generally used to hold criminals in prison, and these were an effective way of taming unruly teenagers. However, such reckless behaviour should stop once the boy has come of age and becomes a 'man'.

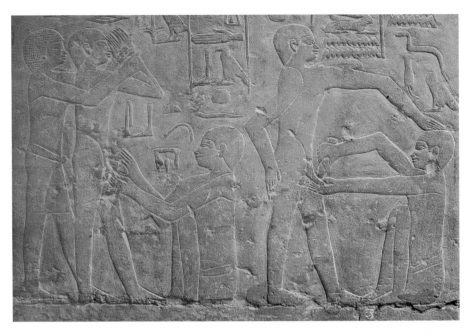

Circumcision scene, Tomb of Ankhmahor. (Photograph courtesy of Werner Forman Archive via Heritage Image Partnership Ltd)

CIRCUMCISION

A boy became a man in his early teens, and this appears to have been marked by a ritual circumcision. There are three images of a circumcision, although only one of them is thought to be of a real event. This appears in the sixth-dynasty Saqqara tomb of Ankhmahor. The boy is firmly held from behind by a servant as a kneeling priest puts ointment on his penis to numb it, saying, 'Hold him firmly. Don't let him swoon.'

The other two images are from divine birth scenes in the temple of Mut at Karnak, and that of Hatshepsut at Deir el Bahri. There are, however, texts which discuss the ritual. On a First Intermediate Period text, a man from Naga ed Dier says, 'When I was circumcised together with 120 men.' This suggests an entire age group was circumcised at the same time, clearly as a public ritual. From the mummies, circumcision is difficult to identify and therefore it is difficult to ascertain how widespread the practice was. It is believed most boys were circumcised in the pharaonic period, although it became less common as time went on.

There is no proof that female circumcision (clitoridectomy) was carried out in ancient Egypt, although one text on the twelfth-dynasty sarcophagus of Sit-

Hedj-Hotep in the Cairo Museum states, 'But if a man wants to live, he should recite it [the spell] every day after his flesh had been rubbed with the Balephd [unknown] of an uncircumcised girl and the flakes of skin of an uncircumcised bald man.' There is some debate whether the word 'uncircumcised' is translated correctly, and could be translated as 'smear'. It is therefore assumed the general rite of passage of girls from childhood to adulthood was when they started their menstrual cycle, or their 'time of purification'. Obviously, this age varied from girl to girl, and whether this was publically acknowledged is unknown.

For both boys and girls, once they made the transition from child to adult their side lock of youth was shaved off. In tomb images children are often presented naked with this side lock, and as soon as they reach adult age they are suddenly represented as miniature adults.

MARRIAGE

One of the first things a young adult did was to get married. There is a misconception that in ancient Egypt sibling marriages were common. This was only for gods, as we saw in chapter 2, and royalty. Royal marriages included brother-sister, father-daughter, or even grandfather-granddaughter marriages. However, these marriages were often political, to reinforce the royal line, and were not always consummated. For ordinary Egyptians, marrying a close relative was unacceptable, although marriages were expected to be between people of the same class and financial background. It is believed that for the elite, marriages may have been arranged by the families, and dowries were paid in these situations. If this was the case a marriage contract was often drawn up.

A Ptolemaic stela in the British Museum belonged to a woman called Taimhotep who married a man over thirty years her senior. In marrying the high priest of Ptah at Memphis, she 'obeyed her father', who was also a high priest of Ptah. This marriage obviously maintained the family's position in society by ensuring she married someone of equal status to her father. The age difference between Taimhotep and Psherenptah may not have been unusual.

Girls often married as soon as they were of childbearing age. As menstrual cycles start at different times for each girl it is possible that girls as young as ten were eligible for marriage. Although boys came of age at approximately twelve years old, often elite boys married after they had started their careers and accumulated enough wealth to maintain a family. Although a boy officially became a man when he was circumcised, socially he was considered an adult once he had obtained his first paid position, whether as a scribe, a soldier or working independently of his father. Therefore this could vary from boy to boy, and from profession to profession. With a hereditary position the boy could be older, when he received the job, than a soldier starting in army, who would have trained as a young child.

Due to this potential age difference it is generally believed that girls were expected to be virgins, to ensure there was no doubt regarding paternity of the first child, but the same was not expected from men.

Many people, where status in society was not so consequential, married for love. However, there were traditions to be upheld even for love matches. The New Kingdom love poetry, although probably written by professional scribes, describes desire and longing for a potential husband or wife. One poem (second stanza of Papyrus Chester Beatty I) laments what appears to be unrequited affection: 'He knows not my wish to embrace him, or he would write to my mother.' This suggests that should a man wish to marry a young woman he was expected to get permission from her mother.

Whether for king or commoner it is rather surprising there was no formal wedding ceremony, either religious or legal. In fact, there was no word in the Egyptian language for 'wedding'. The texts are also silent on wedding celebrations until the Ptolemaic period Story of Setne Khamwas (I), which tells the story of Ahwere and her brother Naneferkaptah, the children of the pharaoh Merenebptah. They loved each other and wished to marry. Initially their father forbade it, as he wanted to expand the family by marrying them to other people. Once he relented, the celebration of the wedding is described thus:

> 'Steward, let Ahwere be taken to the house of Naneferkaptah tonight and let all sorts of beautiful things be taken with her.' I was taken as a wife to the house of Naneferkaptah [that night and Pharaoh] sent me a present of silver and gold, and all Pharaoh's household sent me presents. Naneferkaptah made holiday with me and he entertained all Pharaoh's household. He slept with me that night and found me [pleasing. He slept with] me again and again, and we loved each other.

Although any ceremonial aspects are not discussed this indicates a party marked the occasion, as well as extravagant gift giving. As there were no legal or religious arrangements, this indicates weddings were purely social events. As with Ahwere and Naneferkaptah, for a couple to get married the woman simply left her parents' home and moved in with her new husband. Whether this was marked by a procession through the streets is not recorded, although it would be unusual for such an event not to be celebrated in some way.

As marriage was easy, with no legal documentation, divorce was also straightforward. To divorce, either party declared 'I divorce you', and the woman left her husband's house to either return to her family's home or set up on her own. Documents were generally only produced for wealthy families where a dowry had been paid upon the wedding. Such documents discussed returning the dowry during a divorce. One document on Papyrus Louvre E7846 (546 BCE) records how the lady Tsendjehuty outlines appropriate property reimbursement should she get divorced from her husband, Iturekh son of Petiese. He promised, if he were to divorce her for another woman, that he would give her maintenance, unless the divorce came about due to her own infidelity, 'the large crime that is (usually) found in a woman'.

Divorce had no stigma attached and a divorced man or woman could remarry. However, evidence indicates that women who divorced after the age of thirty-five did not often remarry. Perhaps they were financially self-sufficient and did not need to marry, or could no longer have children, had children already, or were not considered good marriage material.

In the case of couples with children divorcing, it is unknown who gained custody. However there is evidence of alimony being paid to an ex-wife. Details from Deir el Medina inform us that the workman Hesysunebef divorced his wife, Hel, following her affair with Paneb. He gave her a small grain ration every month, which was not enough to make her self-sufficient but no doubt helped. When they divorced, he tried to sell her low-quality scarf on the east bank at the market for her, but no one wanted to buy it. He therefore gave her six times the value for it out of his own income. The information we have about Hel indicates the divorce was her fault, as it is recorded that before she married Hesysunebef she was married to Pendua. Their divorce came about after an earlier affair with Paneb, the same man named in Hesysunebef's divorce documents. One cannot help wondering why she did not marry Paneb.

HOMOSEXUALITY

Not everyone chose to marry, and there is evidence of homosexuality. In Chapter 125 of the Book of the Dead it is stated, 'I have not committed adultery, I have not been unchaste ... I have not done wrong sexually or committed homosexuality.'

This indicates homosexuality was not approved of and therefore needed to be included in this negative confession.

In the Contendings of Horus and Seth, the homosexual encounters between Horus and Seth are always instigated by Seth, the god of chaos (see chapter 2):

> Seth said to Horus 'How beautiful are your buttocks, how vital! Stretch out your legs.' Horus said 'Wait that I may tell it …' Horus said to his mother Isis, 'Seth wants to know me.' She said to him, 'Take care. Do not go near him for that. Next time he mentions it to you, you shall say to him; "It is too difficult because of my build, as you are heavier than I am. My strength is not the same as yours."' She says, 'When he has aroused you, place your fingers between your buttocks … the seed which has come forth from his penis without letting the sun see it.'

Isis, rather than totally discouraging the action, tells Horus what to do once he has been aroused, indicating Seth is the problem, not the homosexual activities.

A Middle Kingdom literary tale tells the story of Pepy II and the General Sasanet and their homosexual relationship. The king is not criticised for having a relationship with a man, nor even for the low status of his lover, but rather for the neglect of his duties while spending four hours every night in pursuit of carnal pleasures.

Niankhkhnum and Khnumhotep embrace in their joint mastaba tomb. Brothers or homosexual partners? (Photograph courtesy of Ahmad Badr, Wikimedia Commons)

The fifth-dynasty mastaba tomb of Niankhkhnum and Khnumhotep has sparked discussion since its discovery in the 1960s as there are rather unusual images of these two men embracing. Due to the nature of the images it has been suggested they were having a homosexual relationship, although wives and children are also represented in the tomb. Perhaps they were brothers or just good friends.

Homosexuality between women, however, was considered to be a bad thing. While being extremely poorly documented, the dream interpretation book on Papyrus Carlsberg states that if a woman 'dreams that a woman has intercourse with her she will come to a bad end'.

Relationships were intended to be procreative so any in which this was not possible was considered to be a waste and was actively discouraged.

CHILDBIRTH

It was considered important in ancient Egypt to have as many children as possible in order to ensure parents were cared for in old age (see chapter 5). Although it was more desirable to have boys so they could take over the father's role and bring a wife into the family who would provide extra care for the elderly, girls were not exposed or abandoned.

For many, the houses were inadequately small, perhaps with three generations living there, meaning it was difficult for newly married couples to be alone. No one had their own bedroom, so at night other people were always present. However, through snatched moments alone, and perhaps through using the box beds in the first room of the house, the woman would generally become pregnant soon after marriage. If this did not happen there were tests to ascertain whether the woman was fertile, although none to check male fertility.

To conceive, it was believed it was necessary to have open passages from the vagina to all body parts, and it was important to test for blockages. The Kahun Gynaecological Papyrus suggests the woman should sit over a concoction of beer and dates. If she vomits, her tubes are open and she will conceive, and if she does not, her tubes are blocked. The number of times she vomited indicated how many children she would have. Another fertility test instructs the woman to insert an onion into her vagina. If the next day her breath smelt of onions she would conceive.

The Berlin and Carlsberg VIII Papyrus provided pregnancy tests which necessitated urinating over barley and emmer seeds. Should the barley sprout first her baby would be a boy, if the emmer sprouted first she would have a girl, but if neither sprouted she was not pregnant. Once pregnancy was established, spells were recited over knotted fabric, which was placed inside the vagina as a tampon. The knot prevented the baby leaving early, and the spell prevented blood from soiling the fabric. However, as there was a very high mortality rate among infants, a woman may have had ten children only half of whom would survive into adulthood. The New Kingdom Instruction of Ani warns, 'Do not say 'I am too young to be taken', for you do not know your death. When death comes he steals the infant who is in his mother's arms, just like him who reached old age.'

Childbirth itself was also a very dangerous time in a woman's life, and many women died during or shortly afterwards. The medical papyri offer numerous remedies to ensure a safe birth for both mother and child. The Kahun Gynaecological Papyrus had remedies for, among other things:

> Causing a woman's womb to go to its place
> Recognising good milk
> To loosen the child in the belly of a woman
> To separate a child from the womb of its mother

The Ebers Papyrus also postulates that should a newborn's first cry be 'ny', he would live, but should it be 'mb', he would die.

The villages of Gurob and Deir el Medina both had a separate cemetery designed especially for babies, with approximately 100 burials, including stillborns, neonatal babies and infants. They were buried in pots, baskets or chests rather than ready-made coffins. Some infants were buried beneath the floors of the houses, sometimes two or three to a box. They were never mummified and were never more than a few months old.

During birth the woman was aided by a midwife. The pregnant woman crouched with her buttocks resting on a sacred birth-brick. This was thought to represent the hieroglyphic sign for horizon, with the baby's head representing the rising son. The few depictions and written descriptions of childbirth indicate that someone stood behind the pregnant woman to support her and the midwife was in front encouraging the birth.

This may have been done with a ceremonial ivory wand engraved with images of Bes, Taweret and other protective deities. Although it is unknown exactly what role it played, it is assumed it may have needed to come into contact with the

Opposite: Hatshepsut's pregnant mother, Deir el Bahri. (Courtesy of BKB Photography)

woman and to remain in the room with her and her baby after birth. A number of them have been found in tombs, ritually broken in two, presumably to prevent the harmful spirits from escaping.

In an attempt to keep mother and baby safe after birth, they were kept secluded in a room called a *hrryt*. In some houses this was a small space beneath the stairs decorated with painted convolvulus leaves, which were semi-erotic fertility symbols. They stayed there for two weeks. In wealthy families where the absence of the women was not so marked, women also confined themselves there during menstruation. It is interesting to note that some of the workmen at Deir el Medina were absent from work because women in their household were menstruating, indicating that he was needed at home during this confinement.

Upon leaving the confinement, the new mother resumed her daily life. She breastfed the child for up to three years as a means of ensuring healthy food for the baby. If the family was wealthy, the mother died in childbirth, or the mother was unable to produce milk, a wet nurse was hired. In the New Kingdom it was a sign of status to have a wet nurse and some officials used the lofty title of milk-brother with the king to show a shared wet nurse.

There was, however, little stigma attached to breastfeeding your own child, and the Papyrus Lansing (a schoolbook) praises the practice by comparing it to that of writing: 'more enjoyable than a mother's giving birth, when her heart knows no distaste. She is constant in nursing her son; her breast is in his mouth every day.'

Not all women wanted to get pregnant again straight after giving birth, and prolonged breastfeeding was thought to prevent this from happening. However, other contraceptives were also available. These included such things as sour milk and crocodile dung. This was inserted into the vagina and the dung acted as an absorbent sponge.

The mother had total responsibility for the children while her husband was at work, bringing us back to where this chapter opened with the discussion of childhood in ancient Egypt.

5

DISEASE, DEATH AND THE AFTERLIFE

The ancient Egyptians, like any civilization, suffered with diseases. Some of these proved to be fatal. Although to the modern eye Egyptian medicine may appear rather primitive, Egyptian doctors were renowned throughout the ancient world for their effectiveness and knowledge, and many of their remedies form the basis of modern medicine.

Despite this, the average lifespan of an ancient Egyptian was short, with women dying at approximately thirty years old, and men at approximately thirty-five years old. However, there were exceptions, with Ramses II (1279–1212 BCE) living well into old age, as did Pepy I (2332–2383 BCE).

Child mortality was extremely high, and many children died in their first year of life. Many more died at the age of three, during the transition from breastfeeding to solid food, but if a child survived this there was a good chance they would survive until adulthood. Although the age of death was so low, the ideal age was 120 years old, and this is often cited in literary tales to show the wisdom of old age. However, reaching such a ripe old age was a dangerous journey, with risks along the way from disease, infection and the doctor's remedies.

WRITTEN EVIDENCE

The main resources for identifying Egyptian diseases are mummies, although evidence for some diseases are not preserved well, and for these we must turn to written records. There are numerous medical papyri listing ailments and the treatment recommended; these may have been consulted by doctors or students.

The Kahun Gynaecological Papyrus, dated from year 29 of Amenemhat III (1825 BCE), was discovered at el Lahun and describes methods of diagnosing pregnancy, the sex of the foetus, toothache during pregnancy, and prescribing feminine drugs, pastes, vaginal applications and contraceptives.

The Old Kingdom Edwin Smith Papyrus is primarily concerned with surgery, describing forty-eight surgical cases of wounds to the head, neck, shoulders, and chest, arranged in order from the head downwards.

The Ebers Papyrus is dated to year 9 of Amenhotep I (1542 BCE), and discusses diseases of the eye, skin and extremities, also gynaecology and surgical diseases. There are 877 recipes and 400 drugs described, which were administered by oral, rectal, vaginal or external applications, or by fumigation.

The rather specialist Chester Beatty VI Papyrus deals solely with diseases of the anus, rectum and bladder, and was discovered at el Lahun. The Hearst Medical Papyrus, like the Ebers, was a general text and covered everything from a 'tooth fallen out' to bites from humans, pigs and hippopotami.

The medical papyri tell us not only about illnesses but also the cures. These remedies were a combination of practical medicine and magic, with incantations being essential for success. The Egyptians, however, saw no difference between the two practices and combined practical medicine with unguents, oils, dancing, music, incantations and laying hands on the patient.

DOCTORS AND THEIR PROFESSION

Primarily doctors were priests, and their favoured deity determined their speciality. As the gods specialised in different things so did the doctors. Herodotus (fifth century BCE) records, 'Medicine is practiced among them on a plan of separation: each physician treats a single disorder and no more.'

GODS AND GODDESSES ASSOCIATED WITH ILLNESSES AND AILMENTS

Sekhmet, the goddess of plagues and epidemics.

Duau, the god of eye diseases.

Taweret and Hathor, goddesses of childbirth.

Horus, the god of deadly stings and bites from crocodiles, snakes and scorpions.

Selqet, the goddess associated with bites and stings from venomous reptiles and insects.

There were also village-based physicians and women who acted as midwives. These women probably learned their craft from their mothers, but were no less valid than a temple-trained physician. Evidence from Deir el Medina also suggests that many villagers self-diagnosed, using the medical papyri as reference, and sent away for the ingredients required. The absentee record shows that Pa-hery-pedjet took a number of days off work to make medicines or 'to be with' someone, and it is assumed he was the village doctor at this time.

If an ailment was obvious, like a wound or broken bone, the prescribed cure was purely medicinal, although often accompanied by an incantation or prayer. If the ailment was internal and the cause was not apparent it was considered to be of supernatural origin, and therefore it was necessary to turn to supernatural means for a cure. However, doctors were continually learning new things about the body and how it worked. The Edwin Smith Papyrus describes knowledge of the pulse: 'It is there that every physician and every priest of Sekhmet places his fingers … he feels something from the heart.' They also knew that the blood supply ran from the heart to all organs in the body: 'It speaks forth in the vessels of every body part.' The Edwin Smith Medical Papyrus describes knowledge of the brain and the connection with paralysis, but they were unaware of the brain's importance in regard to thought processes and emotions.

Although their knowledge was advanced, their medical equipment was not. Discovered in a Saqqara tomb (sixth dynasty), and belonging to the 'Senior Physician of the Royal Palace', Qar, was a complete set of surgical tools.

SET OF SURGICAL TOOLS BELONGING TO QAR

A rush (used with a knife for cutting treatments)
A fire drill (to burn growths)
Knife/chisel
Cupping glass
Thorn (to burst blisters)
Heated broken glass – for eye treatments
Swaps, tampons, linen material
Knives, salve spoons, and mortars

The medical procedure was very well defined in the Ebers Papyrus and was similar to modern practice. The doctor starts by asking the patient about the problem, before conducting a physical examination which included a study of urine, stools, sputum and blood, before checking the pulse: 'You should put your finger on it, you should examine the belly.' The final test was reflexes: 'Examine his belly and knock on his finger ... Place your hand on the patient and tap.' Once the full examination was complete the doctor made a diagnosis, which was one of three decisions: 'An ailment which I will treat,' 'An ailment which I will contend,' or 'An ailment not to be treated.' Only fourteen out of forty-eight cases on Ebers were considered hopeless.

The prescriptions were prescribed with dosage according to age: 'If it is a big child, he should swallow it like a draught, if he is still in swaddles, it should be rubbed by his nurse in milk and thereafter sucked on four days.'

The time of day the treatment was most effective was specified: 'And the eye is painted therewith in the evening its other half is dried, finely ground, and the eye is painted therewith in the morning.'

The duration of the prescription is particularly important and the Ebers Papyrus specifies the number of days whereas the Edwin Smith describes the patient's condition: 'Until he recovers,' 'Until the period of his injury passes by,' or 'Until you know that he has reached a decision point.'

Medical instruments. Kom Ombo.
(Photograph courtesy of Dennis Jarvis,
Wikimedia Commons)

Many of the medicines prescribed were applied logically, with medicines taken orally for internal diseases, external applications for pain, ointments for skin diseases, inhalations for respiratory diseases, gargles for mouth disorders, baths and douches for gynaecological problems and enemas for intestinal infections. For example, a remedy for burns on the Ebers Papyrus comprised 'barley bread, oil/fat and salt, mixed into one. Bandage with it often to make him well immediately.' For sufferers of cataracts, the cure was a mixture of 'brain of tortoise with honey'. While this was being applied, a prayer was spoken asking gods to remove this darkness from the eye.

Some of the ingredients contained properties still considered useful in modern medicine. For example, the Edwin Smith Papyrus describes cleaning a wound before it is stitched up with needle and thread. It recommends applying raw meat to the wound on the first day. Meat has an active enzyme which facilitates healing. Other drugs contained anti-bacterial or antiseptic ingredients such as honey, frankincense, cinnamon, willow leaves, acacia or fir oil.

As the Egyptian environment was dusty, exacerbated by regular sandstorms, many people suffered from a disease called sand pneumoconiosis. It is similar to the disease suffered by coal miners and stone masons, and therefore was prevalent among tomb craftsmen. It caused shortness of breath and severe coughs. There was no cure other than inhaling honey, cream, carob, and date kernels.

Headaches were common and there are twelve remedies recorded, one of which consists of a poultice of 'fruit of coriander made into a mass, honey is mixed with it, the head is bandaged therewith so that it goes immediately well with him'.

The common cold, however, had a religious incantation instead of a practical medicinal application. The doctor needed to recite, 'Flow out fetid nose! Flow out son of fetid nose. Flow out, you who break the bones, destroy the skull, and make ill the seven holes of the head.' (Ebers Papyrus)

There were of course ailments that are simply not identified in the medical papyri, although the symptoms are. The most common was infestation by parasitic worms, attested by numerous mummies. All mummies studied by the Manchester Mummy Project have shown evidence of at least one parasitic worm, some as many as three, showing how common they were.

The most common in ancient and modern Egypt is bilharzia (schistosomiasis), caused by the *Schistsoma haematobia* worm, released by the water snail. It penetrates intact skin, entering the veins and resulting in anaemia, loss of appetite, urinary infection, and loss of resistance to other diseases. Blood in the urine was the most common symptom and there are two columns of remedies on the Ebers Papyrus for this. As many Egyptians worked in stagnant water in the fields and marshes, they came in contact with the water snail and bilharzia easily.

Water supplies were easily infected with other worms if situated near latrines or stagnant water. Mummy 1770 in the Manchester Museum shows remains of the Guinea worm, contracted through drinking water infected with a small crustacean containing immature forms of the parasite, which then developed in the stomach. The male was preserved in the calcium of the mummy's abdomen. The female normally settles in the legs, causing ulcers, allowing eggs to be passed out of the body and into the water supply. This mummy's legs were amputated shortly before her death, although it is not thought to be as a result of this infestation.

The body of the weaver Nakht (twentieth dynasty) had bilharzia, *Trichnella* and *Taenia*. *Trichnella* is contracted by eating undercooked pork containing immature forms of the worm. These develop in the intestine and the female deposits up to 1,500 larvae, which can travel into every organ of the body. *Taenia* is caught through undercooked beef or pork. Nakht may have suffered with fever, muscle pain and weakness.

A much easier ailment for the doctors to deal with was a broken bone, and mummies show breaks to the forearm and leg which had healed completely, indicating they were set correctly in splints. Plaster casts were either made from cow's milk mixed with barley, or acacia leaves mixed with gum and water smeared over the break. One skeleton discovered in 2013 at Amarna had suffered from a broken foot and femur, and was one of two skeletons wearing a copper alloy toe ring, the only such items discovered in Egypt. It is thought they may have been worn to aid healing.

DENTAL CARE

While we have the names and titles of more than 100 doctors, only seven also held the title of dentist. However, a dentist's role was not preventative or interventional but dealt purely with the symptoms of dental problems.

The Egyptians generally suffered from extreme tooth wear brought on by collagen in meats, cellulose and silica structures in plants and sand in the flour. In some instances the enamel was completely destroyed, exposing the sensitive inner pulp. Wear of this nature affected both rich and poor members of society. Pliny (23–79 CE) suggested sand or powdered brick was intentionally added by the Carthaginians when grinding corn to facilitate the grinding process, and the same could be true in Egypt. Experiments have shown that grinding corn for fifteen minutes caused very little change, whereas adding a handful of sand produced fine flour very quickly. Evidence of quartz, greywacke, amphibole and mica grains have been discovered in bread examples, all possibly added to make grinding easier.

A common ailment, possibly an indirect symptom of tooth attrition, was dislocation and marked osteoarthritic changes to the jaw. The Edwin Smith Papyrus describes the remedy for this: 'When you examine a man with a lower jaw that is displaced, and you find his mouth open, so that you cannot close his mouth; then you should put your finger on the end of both jaw bones in the inside of his mouth, and put your thumbs under his chin; then you must let them (the displaced joint bone) fall together in their places ... bandage them with the *imr.w* [unknown] and honey every day until he is better.'

The most common consequence of such extreme tooth wear and exposed dental pulp were abscesses. Studies by the Manchester Mummy Project showed that in twenty-nine male bodies there were seventy-two abscesses and in twelve females studied there were forty-five abscesses. This was clearly a widespread problem, with many people having more than one. Treatment was limited to pain relief or draining: 'a disease that I treat with a knife treatment. If anything remains in pocket, it recurs' (Ebers Papyrus). To drain an abscess the physician cut it and let the pus drain out. Sometimes the doctors were too late and the abscess had started to destroy the jaw bone as it created a path to eject the pus. Some human remains show the teeth almost falling out of abscess cavities, indicating dentists did not perform extractions. The Ebers Papyrus suggests using bitter apple (*Colocynth*), cumin, turpentine (*Terebinth*), cow's milk, earth almonds and evening dew as painkillers. In some cases these cures may have made the infection worse.

While suffering greatly from wear to the teeth and its associated problems, the Egyptians had very few caries (decay), as their diet was low in sugar. However, a change of diet in the Ptolemaic period to one high in sugar and carbohydrates saw an increase in dental caries. The Egyptians believed caries were formed by the tunnelling of the *fnt*-worm, or tooth worm. There is no evidence that fillings were used, and so they simply continued to grow until they reached the inner pulp of the teeth, allowing bacteria to get into the tooth and forming abscesses.

An important piece of dentistry evidence was a dental bridge discovered in a fourth-dynasty mastaba (tomb), although the reuse of the mastaba in the

Ptolemaic period casts doubt over the date. The bridge was between an incisor and a canine, and calculus on the canine and associated teeth indicated the bridge had been worn for some time. The central incisor also had a groove on the labial side to accommodate the wire comfortably within the mouth.

The ancient Egyptians did try preventative dental care in the form of toothbrushes made of the frayed end of a twig, as the highly polished appearance of the teeth of mummies suggests. They also used cinnamon breath fresheners and chewed on natron to cleanse the mouth. Cloves were used for pain relief, as were beans ground up with willow. Willow forms the basis of modern aspirin and may therefore have worked.

Despite the number of people suffering with extremely painful dental problems, the absentee records from Deir el Medina show there were no days off for toothache. Perhaps their pain threshold was higher than ours today, or the pain was considered normal.

OLD AGE

By the age of thirty-five an ancient Egyptian was considered elderly, and although it came earlier than in modern times, the concept of old age has remained the same. The opening paragraph of the Instruction of Ptahhotep (fifth dynasty) describes old age:

> Old age is here, high age has arrived,
> Feebleness came, weakness grows,
> Childlike one sleeps all day.
> Eyes are dim, ears are deaf,
> Strength is waning, one is weary,
> The mouth silence, speaks not
> The heart, void, recalls not the past
> The bones ache throughout

Although Ptahhotep emphasises the physicality of old age, the wisdom of old age was also greatly revered. In a community with no state-run care system, it was essential for people to have many children in order for someone to provide for them in old age. In a situation where a couple were childless it was not unusual to adopt an orphan or an older individual who then had the responsibility of taking care of their adoptive parents. It is difficult to identify whether there was an official adoption system, as the same terminology was used for adoption of a child or an apprentice. However, the implications were the same. It was the filial duty to be a 'staff of old age', and without children an elderly man or woman could be rendered helpless within the village.

Some children played the role well, and one son, Weskhetnemtet, after taking over his father's role gave half his rations to his father for ten months. However, not all children were as accommodating. The last will of Naunakhte (twentieth dynasty), shows how she disinherited four of her nine children because they did not look after her in old age as she expected them to. Her will lists in minute detail what she planned to leave to the other children, who provided for her adequately.

This duty to care for the elderly became embroiled in religion, and in the tomb biographies it often states, 'I have provided for the widow who had no husband … I provided for the old one while I gave him my staff, causing the old woman to say "That is good."' (Tomb of Rekhmire, TT100). These biographies emphasised the good deeds of the deceased to facilitate their entry into the afterlife. Helping widows was also included in many of the Wisdom Texts, which outlined ideal behavioural conduct. One such text, written on an ostracon in the Petrie Museum, emphasises 'You should not mock an old man or woman when they are decrepit. Beware lest they take action against you before you get old.'

However, this advice did not prevent people making fun of the elderly. The Turin Erotic Papyrus depicts a New Kingdom Theban brothel, where the clients (or client, as it is uncertain if they are all the same man or not) are balding and likely to be elderly. At the start of the papyrus the man is enthusiastic, but as his adventures continue he becomes exhausted, with one scene showing him with a huge erect penis lying under the bed while the young woman above tries to entice him into her arms. In the next scene he is carried away by two young girls, his penis flaccid.

In the Tomb Robbery Papyri in the British Museum, a man called Shedsukhons shows frustration with his elderly father, who interfered in the division of spoils: 'O doddering old man, evil be his old age; if you are killed and thrown into the water who will look for you?'

PENSIONS

While the majority of the elderly were at the mercy of the kindness of their children or strangers, a state pension was provided for the workmen at Deir el Medina, soldiers and their commanding officers. Records at Deir el Medina showing the amount of grain distributed on a monthly basis mention a ration going to a few widows and workmen described as 'old'. These provisions were less than the average wage, but adequate to live on.

Soldiers received land as part of their salary under the proviso that they would be available for work whenever needed. The yield from this land could be maintained as a form of pension once they were too old to fight. Favoured officials were often given an honorary priestly or administrative title by the king, allowing a salary but with no work attached. A Theban official, Nebamun (TT90), for example, was given the position of Chief of Police by Thutmosis IV: 'Now My Majesty has ordered to appoint him to be police chief on the West of the City of Thebes, in the places Tembu and Obau, until he will reach the blessed state (of the dead).' The provision of this role until death indicates it was in title only, and was therefore a pension post.

When the time came, one of the most important things a child (eldest son) could do for his parents was to provide them with a decent burial as well as 'keep their name alive' through voice offerings and prayers. The Egyptians were worried that should these rituals not be carried out adequately they would not

Anubis, the god of embalming. Deir el Medina.

CANOPIC EQUIPMENT

The organs removed from the body during the mummification process were also dried in natron and wrapped, before being placed into canopic jars. These were a set of four jars, each lid in a different shape, representative of the four sons of Horus. Each son had a specific role in the protection of the organ within. The stomach was placed in the jar with the jackal head (Duamutef), the intestines with the hawk-headed jar (Qebusenuef), the lungs in the jar with the baboon head (Hapy), and the liver with the human-headed jar (Imsety). These were then placed in the tomb, either in their own room if the tomb was big enough, or close to the coffin.

enter the afterlife and they would be destined for oblivion. According to the Westcar Papyrus, 'old age is the time of death, enwrapping, and burial'.

Mummification and the elaborate burial practices have often led to the belief that the Egyptians were obsessed with death, whereas in fact it was an obsession with life and its continuation. This rested on the belief that after death the deceased continued to live in the afterlife. The afterlife looked a lot like Egypt, with a central river and fields of crops in abundance. They were buried with all their possessions as they needed these things in the afterlife when they were reborn. The most important possession, of course, was their body, as without a body it may be impossible to be reborn at all.

MUMMIFICATION

Strangely enough we have no records of how the mummification process was carried out. The earliest written record comes from Herodotus (fifth century BCE), although earlier tomb images depict some of the funerary rituals. However, the mummification process was considered too mundane or well known to record. Therefore we have to use Herodotus in conjunction with the mummies themselves in order to understand the process.

Mummification was carried out by priests who held a high status within the community. The high priest was responsible for the wrapping, and wore an Anubis mask during the process. Anubis was the god of embalming, and guided the deceased into the afterlife. The embalmers worked on the west bank of the Nile in a temporary structure called the Pure Place, which may also have acted as a showroom, allowing the embalmers to display their work for potential customers.

Mummification was only for the wealthy, although there were three options available. The most expensive was designed to create an 'Osiris' of the deceased. The process started when the body was brought to the embalmers and washed.

In the New Kingdom they then removed the brain, as it was believed to be superfluous to requirements. All thought processes and emotions were thought to have happened in the heart rather than the brain. To remove it, the ethmoid bone at the top of the nose was broken, and the brain was removed in pieces using a hooked instrument. Experiments have shown this method was inefficient for removing the whole organ. An alternative method necessitated pouring juniper oil and turpentine up the nose, dissolving the brain, which was then poured out through the nostrils.

The mouth was cleansed and packed with resin, and a paste also made from resin was applied to the face. Next, a cut was made in the left side of the abdomen using a flint knife, enabling the embalmer to remove all internal organs except the heart. The removed organs were preserved, wrapped and placed in canopic jars.

The body cavity was cleaned with palm wine and an infusion of pounded spices, which prevented it smelling. The abdomen was then stuffed with bundles of natron, wrapped in linen, and left to dry, along with the rest of the body. Once it had dried out the cavity was filled with a mixture of aromatic substances and linen or sawdust to give it shape. The hole in the side was sewn up and the wound hidden with a bronze or leather cover.

Once the organs were removed and the cavity packed with natron packages, the body was placed in natron. Depending on the size of the body, the drying took between thirty-five and forty days.

A recent experiment carried out at Sheffield University suggested that in the eighteenth dynasty, instead of covering the body in natron, the bodies were submerged in a salt bath, which infused the soft tissues themselves with the salt solution, preserving them from the inside. After four weeks in the solution and two weeks drying, a mummy was formed. This part of the process took forty-two days, not including the removal of the internal organs, meaning twenty-eight days remained to complete the wrapping of the body.

The wrapping of the body would normally take between thirty and thirty-five days, giving a total of seventy days for the whole process.

WRAPPING THE BODY

Wrapping the body was as important as the preservation, and an Anubis priest oversaw the process. As each limb was wrapped it was essential to recite the appropriate prayers in order to turn the limb into a divine object. There were numerous layers of bandages, with one second-dynasty mummy having sixteen intact layers remaining of what may have been thirty original layers. In the Middle Kingdom, between each layer of bandages was a sheet to provide extra padding. Anything up to 400 square metres of linen was used to wrap the mummy. Between all of these layers of bandages the priests laid protective amulets, each in a designated place with a specific set of prayers and incantations attached to them.

To make the body appear more lifelike, pads of linen were placed to emulate breasts, and in the twenty-first dynasty they went so far as to make slits behind the knees, ankles, and heels in order to place folded linen pads under the skin,

Tombs in the cliffs surrounding Deir el Bahri, Luxor.

ensuring the body shape was not lost. While the eyeballs were not removed, as the body dried they sank into the head, so often false ones were placed beneath the eyelids. These were made of faience, linen, or even onions in the case of the mummy of Ramses IV.

With such a large amount of linen needed for each body, many of the bandages were recycled household linen. Royalty, however, had custom-made bandages and some of Ramses II's were woven from blue and gold thread. In the later periods, funerary texts from the Book of the Dead were written on the bandages to aid the deceased in the afterlife.

The whole mummification process took seventy days, to reflect the time Osiris disappeared before he was reborn in the afterlife. This is associated with the observation that the star Sirius, closely associated with Osiris, disappeared for a period of seventy days. However, there were instances when the burial process took more or less time. In the fourth-dynasty Giza tomb of Queen Meresankh III, it is recorded she was buried 272 days after her death. Another inscription, belonging to a Ptolemaic high priest of Memphis, states he was buried 200 days

Funeral of Ramose, showing mourners and the procession of funerary goods. The top register shows the coffin being dragged to the tomb. (Photograph courtesy of David Schmid, Wikimedia Commons)

Solar barque, Denderah. (Photograph courtesy of BKB Photography)

after his death. Conversely, in the absentee records of Deir el Medina it is indicated that sometimes it was only a matter of a few days between death and burial.

The reasons for such extended delay are unrecorded, although political instability may have been an important factor. Equally the reasons for quick burials are also unrecorded, although it is possible that cheaper mummification may have been quicker.

MUMMIFICATION ON A BUDGET

Cheaper mummification processes became available in the Middle Kingdom when mummification for non-royals became popular. These did not involve the removal of the internal organs. Instead a mixture of cedar oil and turpentine was injected into the body through the anus, which was stopped up to prevent the liquid escaping. The body was then packed in natron for forty days.

After forty days the dissolved organs were drained out through the anus. Some mummies have blocked rectums where the organs have not dissolved fully. Experiments on dead rabbits show the only organ that did not dissolve using this method was the heart, which was convenient as this was normally intentionally left in place.

Then the body was washed and prepared for wrapping. The cheapest option meant the body was returned unwrapped to the family. Evidence suggests once the mummies were returned to the family, they were not buried straight away and remained in the family home for some time until the family tomb was opened; either annually or bi-annually.

The Afterlife

If the tomb scenes are to be believed, the funeral was a big event with a long procession, comprising servants carrying goods to go into the tomb, the coffin, professional mourners wailing and throwing dirt over themselves and the family walking serenely at the back. The longer the procession of goods and the louder the mourners, the more impressive the funeral was considered.

A good funeral was essential in ensuring the deceased entered the afterlife. The non-royal population entered the Field of Reeds, the Egyptian equivalent of heaven, for eternity, doing whatever they wanted to do with no restrictions of health or wealth. The Field of Reeds was the exact replica of Egypt, with a river and fertile fields in abundance.

The king, on the other hand, joined the sun god upon his solar barque and travelled the underworld for twelve hours until he was reborn at dawn. This nocturnal environment was hostile, filled with demons and enemies whose sole purpose was to destroy the solar barque and prevent the sun (and therefore the king) from being reborn in the morning.

Reaching the afterlife was difficult for everyone and relied on the unification of the six elements of the human psyche; if one of them failed the afterlife was unobtainable. The six elements were:

1. The physical body preserved through the process of mummification.
2. The name, repeated in prayers and offerings after death.
3. The shadow, which was a spiritual element indicative of the presence and protection of the sun.
4. The *ba* was the personality of the deceased and was represented as a bird with a human face. This element only appears after death and can travel away from the body.

5. The *ka* was the life force of the deceased and was the element that needed to be nourished with food offerings. This is present throughout the deceased's entire life.

6. The *akh* (spirit) was formed through the *ba* and *ka*. This spirit was powerful and was almost divine in nature.

The unification of these six elements was facilitated by the Opening of the Mouth ceremony, where the oldest son of the deceased held an adze to the mouth of the mummy, enabling them to speak, hear and smell. The *ka* could now enjoy the food and drink offerings and the deceased could hear and participate in temple rituals. The deceased was now ready to endure the final test before entering the afterlife.

This was the Weighing of the Heart Ceremony in the Hall of Judgement, where the deceased stood before Osiris, the god of the underworld, to witness his heart being weighed against Maat, the feather of truth. If the heart was heavier it was devoured by the monster Ammit, waiting nearby. Rather than leaving this to chance, the deceased recited the Negative Confession, Chapter 125 of the Book of the Dead, telling the gods of the underworld the things he/she had not done:

> I have done no falsehood
> I have not robbed
> I have not been rapacious
> I have not stolen
> I have not killed men
> I have not destroyed food supplies

If anything was missed from this list the Egyptians placed an amulet called a heart scarab over the heart, with a prayer encouraging the scarab not to betray the sins still present in the heart.

If the heart weighed the same as the feather of truth, the deceased was reborn and could enter the Field of Reeds for eternity. However it was essential that offerings of food and drink were continually made and their names repeated. Many tombs therefore have an inscription encouraging passers-by to recite the names of the deceased, enabling them to live for eternity: 'Oh, you who live and exist, who like life and hate death, whosoever shall pass by this tomb, as you love life and hate death so you offer to me what is in your hands.' (Middle Kingdom stela from Abydos, now in Cairo)

WHAT NEXT?

BOOKS

Booth, C. (2010) *The Nile and its People*. Stroud. The History Press.

Booth, C. (2007) *Ancient Egyptians for Dummies*. Bognor Regis. John Wiley.

Clayton, P. (1994) *Chronicle of the Pharaohs*. London. Thames and Hudson.

David, R. (2002) *Religion and Magic in Ancient Egypt*. London. Penguin.

Dodson, A. and S. Ikram (1998) *The Mummy in Ancient Egypt; Equipping the Dead for Eternity*. London. Thames and Hudson.

Hart, G. (1986) *A Dictionary of Egyptian Gods and Goddesses*. London. Routledge.

Janssen, R. and J. Janssen (1990) *Growing Up in Ancient Egypt*. London. Rubicon Press.

Janssen, R. and J. Janssen (1996) *Getting Old in Ancient Egypt*. London. Rubicon Press.

Lurker, M. (1974) *The Gods and Symbols of Ancient Egypt*. London. Thames and Hudson.

Manniche, L. (1997) *Sexual Life in Ancient Egypt*. London. Kegan Paul Press.

Quirke, S. (1992) *Ancient Egyptian Religion*. London. British Museum Press.

Robins, G. (1993) *Women in Ancient Egypt*. London. British Museum Press.

Shaw, I. and P. Nicholson (1995) *British Museum Dictionary of Ancient Egypt*. London. British Museum Press.

Wilkinson, R. H. (2003) *The Complete Gods and Goddesses of Ancient Egypt*. London. Thames and Hudson.

MAGAZINES

Ancient Egypt Magazine, Manchester, http://ancientegyptmagazine.co.uk.

Ancient Planet Magazine, Greece, http://ancientplanet.blogspot.co.uk.

Egyptian Archaeology, London, http://www.ees.ac.uk/publications/egyptian-archaeology.html.

Kmt, a modern journal of ancient Egypt, Sebastapol California, http://www.kmtjournal.com.

WEBSITES

The Amarna Project: www.amarnaproject.com. The official website of the excavations carried out at Amarna.

Digital Egypt: www.digitalegypt.ucl.ac.uk. Information about the material culture of ancient Egypt based at the Petrie Museum.

Egypt Exploration Society: ees.ac.uk. An Egyptology organisation which has an archive and runs excavations to Egypt.

The Griffith Institute, Oxford: www.griffith.ox.ac.uk/perl/gi-ca-qsearch.pl. An Egyptology archive.

Theban Mapping Project: www.thebanmappingproject.com. The official website of the work that has been carried out in Thebes.

INDEX

Forthcoming Illustrated Introductions

Fascinated by history? Wish you knew more?
The Illustrated Introductions are here to help.

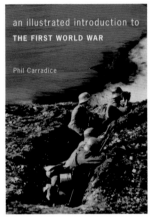

An Illustrated Introduction to the
First World War
978-1-4456-3296-4
£9.99
Available from June 2014

An Illustrated Introduction to the
Second World War
978-1-4456-3848-5
£9.99
Available from August 2014

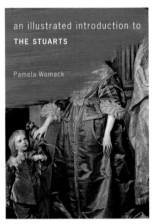

An Illustrated Introduction to the Stuarts
978-1-4456-3788-4
£9.99
Available from September 2014

Available from all good bookshops or to order direct
Please call **01453-847-800**
www.amberleybooks.com